Meynell Games on. . .

PARACHUTE Play

Written by Meynell
with help from many others

Meynell Games Publications

London

Copyright © 1993 by Meynell
Copyright © 1996 by Meynell

ISBN 1 898068 00 3

First published August 1993
Second Edition [minor changes] June 1996

Conditions of Sale:
Whilst the copyright for this book remains with Meynell this copy is sold with permission for the purchaser to use it in any way that they see fit including copying and lending out, but excluding resale, or for any fund generating purpose. The author requests that when extracts and copies are used, acknowledgement be given to Meynell Games by using a phrase similar to: "This was originally in a book called Meynell Games on. . . Parachute Play". Copies of the book are also available in disk format.

British Library Cataloguing-in-Publication Data

A catalogue record for this book is available from the British Library

Meynell Games Publications
10 Grove Road, North Finchley
London N12 9DY
0181 446 5551

Printed and bound in Great Britain by FOTODIRECT LIMITED

This book is dedicated to my mummy,
Mollie Walter. She has encouraged me
and supported me - and spoils me rotten
when I stay with her!!

Acknowledgements

There are many people who have helped in one way or another in making this book happen. In addition to all those who have come out to run and help at parachute sessions for Meynell Games since 1985, I would also like specifically to draw attention to the following:

Kevin Blake	The only person to have played cat and mouse continually for 3½ hours.
Peter Marks	Who invented the phrase "This game is a favourite at Meynell Games" - meaning I'm thinking this one up as I go along.
Roger Marks	He once or twice came out to play but is also a good friend with ideas and help.
Mike Lassman	A very good friend who gives support, help and when really needed his time and body too!
Nick Joseph	He played parachute games live - on radio!! He also gives lots of support and ideas and is still playing today.
Jo Djora	Who started when I started the organisation and has played and grown ever since.
Tina Elliot	A major force behind wanting the book when I started it in 1983, she even typed up the first draft.
Irvin Feldman	The single most significant force in my development - thank you.
Cliff Cohen	My first mentor in youth work; he may have moved on to other things but I don't forget him.
Myra Topper	A colleague who taught me that I could use my voice and not be afraid.
Stephen Cotsen	My friend and my twin - words of encouragement and songs for support.
Rachel Barrow	A solid and thorough administrative worker and friend. She did the bulk of the work for this book.
Lee Wax	A friend throughout.
Karen Frank	A friend who stayed up late, helped me through the stress of turning ideas and concepts into the written word and encouraged me to get it finished. She was there when I really needed her!
The Originals	This group of people came as a team to work and learn in Aberdeen - I taught them and they taught me. In the first year it was Mike Sacker, Adele Simons and Neil Marcus and the second group included Paul Solomon, Yvette Mindel and Tanya Stebbings
Naomi Franks	My sister, who has a significant interest in all that happens.
KVG	She has been with me for a long time and still plays.
Penny Rabiger	She also has been with me for a long time and still plays.
Sarah Montague	One of those who was there at the beginning and who still plays.
Sophie, Big & Monty	For letting Russ come out to play (as if they could have stopped him!)
Ben Gross	The wild man.
Games Teams	Because whenever they work they inspire me.
Colin Bulka	A colleague who shared concepts and skills.
Louis Levy	He's never actually worked for me but he has always been around.
Steve Bull	The Sports Psychologist who helps me turn actual play into theoretical reality.
David Pelham	For constant advice, help, support - and proof reading!
Tony Harris	Who as well as being an occasional member of the games team has provided a great deal of advice and support in the purchase and development of my computer systems.

CONTENTS

Introduction

My name is Meynell and I have been playing with parachutes since the mid '70s. In 1983 I decided to share my ideas with the world at large [how very egotistical!] by writing a book designed to expose my philosophy and approach to games playing.

Well, that book never happened although I did start to write it and many people saw the draft; but what did happen was that I started to concentrate on sharing my excitement and enjoyment of parachute games. I wrote my degree thesis and realised that a real book would be no harder! So to push me on my way we established the publishing company — "Meynell Games Publications" — and this parachute book is the first publication.

There have been hurdles along the way, both technical and mental, but finally the book is produced, late, but I hope nevertheless welcomed.

How to use this book

When I first had the idea, I wanted to produce a book that someone with little or no experience of parachute play could pick up and within minutes be capable of running a games session. I do believe that with the book in one hand and the parachute in the other and a group of responsive young people around the canopy, anyone could run a successful session.

Each page is designed with eight different sections:

1. Name

These are the names that I use. I recognise that other people call the same games by different names. Indeed other staff within Meynell Games use different names and I'm sure you will too — it doesn't matter. You only need the name so that you are reminded of the game.

2. Ages

In reality almost any game will work with almost any age. Some of the more complex games take much longer to explain and to be effective with younger participants you do need a very willing and cooperative group; so you may choose to target ages appropriately.

Some games seem too 'babyish' for older participants but with the appropriate encouragement they will soon be totally involved.

3. Numbers

Obviously different sizes of parachutes can be used with different numbers of players. For the purposes of the book I have worked, loosely, with a 24 ft canopy. Like so many other concepts and practices in play work, that which works well for me is likely to be very different for you. So, please, look on these numbers only as rough guidelines. Indeed, for many games when I have indicated that there is no maximmum number of participants you will find through experience the best numbers. This also varies with the ages of those participating.

4. ENERGY LEVEL

I selected five purely arbitrary names for different energy levels:

Mellow — relaxed, gentle games

Calm — like the sea only more so.

Active — requires some energy and movement, but nothing too energetic.

Hyper — your heart rate will increase, these games are energetic.

Wild — for the fit, dynamic, lively sort of people, who just don't care.

Some games will confuse you with an energy level like calm/hyper. These are games that start slowly and grow!

5. SCRIPT

These are the words I use when I'm running the game. The problem is that if you are not careful and you use my words without being dynamic and exciting, you could end up speaking in a very patronising voice and manner.

When I talk, I try to be excited, enthusiastic, and encouraging and if I ever sound patronising then I hope that someone will tell me so that I can change.

6. BASIC RULES

If you are the sort of person who just wants a set of rules to read and will then develop the game from there, these are for you. I have tried in a few short sentences to explain the game.

7. SAFETY

In principle parachute games are safe activities, but like all safe activities there are ways in which accidents, however small, can happen. Different ages of group, diffferent attitudes of participants and different sizes of groups will all effect the safety aspects of the games. Please read the safety section and always remember that if you are not happy with the safety level then do not play the game.

8. MEYNELL SAYS...

For some of the games I wanted to add a comment that I thought would be useful, helpful, or funny. This is they!

9. OWN NOTES

This is for you. Keep notes of variations, how well it works with different groups, what you would do differently next time; this space is for you to help improve your skills. If you want you could send us your variations to be included in any future editions or updates!

The Photos

Opposite each game is a photograph of it in action. As you can imagine, obtaining photos to represent a dynamic ongoing activity has been very difficult. I have chosen photos that either show the game in 'action' or which demonstrate a specific part of the game.

I hope that these photos do help you when you are confused.

The photos were not taken within the setting of a 'proper' games session but rather with a number of school pupils in a gymnasium. I felt that by staging a photo session that I would be better able to produce pictures that reflected the games.

I am very grateful for the help given to me for the photo session by the staff and pupils at St. Wilfrid's R. C. Senior Secondary School in Crawley and particularly the Head teacher Bernard Smith, the staff of the Physical Education department [Mr. Turner and Miss Frank] and the pupils of 9T, 9C, 9S, 10F, 10M, 10S, 10T, and 10A who wanted to be famous!

Indexing

At the end of the book I have attempted to provide some useful indexing. I have indexed the contents in 2 ways:

Alphabetically by name of game

By energy level

Play Canopies and Parachutes

When writing this book I decided that everyone should be using a 24 ft parachute canopy. If you are using a larger one, the games are identical but you can involve more people. With a smaller canopy you may find that some of the games do not work as you would wish.

There are now a great variety of canopies and a wide range of prices in the market place. I believe that there are most sizes available from 12 ft to 28 ft and some of these are manufactured play canopies whilst others are ex flight parachute canopies.

If you are not buying one of the larger parachute canopies from Meynell Games I would suggest that you make sure that whatever you buy is a circular canopy with a central hole and made in triangular-ish segments. My experience has shown that if you buy anything else you may as well be playing with an old blanket! I also believe that genuine ex-flight parachutes in good condition will last longer and play harder than many of the play canopies that are on sale today. [However, it is only with play canopies that you will get a guarantee against faulty manufacture.]

So You Think You Can Be A Playworker?

And having the willingness and the enthusiasm is half way there!

No-one is born a natural playworker. Whilst some people have strong skills, we all need to study and train in order to develop and grow, and to discover the most effective ways of working with young people.

We must remember to think and be aware of the way we talk to young people, the way we value young people, the way we use touch with young people and we must ensure that at all times our actions are appropriate.

We must remember "Children are real people too" and that it is inappropriate to belittle them or talk down to them, even in fun. We should always treat children and young people in a way similar to that in which we would wish to be treated.

We must remember that through our work we must strive to ensure that we do not perpetuate or promote any racist, sexist or heterosexist stereotypes, and that we must be prepared to challenge them when we hear children or colleagues doing so.

When playing the games it is important to make each one 'your own'. Yes, use the script to help you become familiar with the game but then move on. As soon as you become comfortable change the words you use and make the script your own. You and I are not the same people and therefore you and I will not run the games in the same way.

One of our biggest fears is of it all going wrong, but I have always believed that if we make a mistake, it doesn't matter, as long as you own up and try something else.

If a game doesn't work — change it! You know when a game isn't working when the participants start to become disruptive or vote with their feet and go elsewhere. In the same vein, if a game is working well, don't be afraid to stay with it. You may have played it many times before; it may be you who are 'bored' not your participants.

When running a session it is important to allow the participants the option of opting out. Whilst we would like all to take part we must recognise that there will be games and times when individuals will just not want to be participating and we must allow them to feel free to say "No, I don't want to take part in this." To accept that statement with the honesty that has been given and not to challenge or degrade the person for saying it; to resist from trying to coerce or push that person back into the cooperative play environment. We encourage people to make choices and when the choice has been made, that is it!

It is very important for you to get yourself in the right frame of mind before going out and starting the session. Although a games session can lift you if you are feeling down, if you are running the games without a smile on your face, looking like death warmed up or generally projecting an 'I don't want to be there' image, then you have a battle on your hands before you start. Your group will feed off your energies and if you are sparking, the group will spark along with you.

When running a session it is important to introduce yourself, your colleagues and your parachute at the beginning of the session, to ask people their names and to refer to them during the session, and when you end to thank you colleagues and the participants for playing with you.

If you are lucky some may thank you but never finish by asking if the group had fun or enjoyed themselves as all this is doing is asking them to praise you!

Some Broader Thoughts on Parachute Play

Starting to Play Together

These games are to help bring individuals together as a group and, as a group, to be able to play together. The emphasis on co-operation means that all the participants will choose to join in. The emphasis on playing together means that each participant will becomes concerned that all the others are participating. The task of the play worker is to reinforce the concept of co-operation by using phrases such as 'Let's do this together', 'Let's watch what the person next to us is doing'. The session facilitator must try to use the 'we' and 'us' when working with a group and not try to isolate themselves by saying 'YOU do this' or 'YOUR job is to...' to the group

Active Games and Competition

There are two sides to this type of play; 1) When the whole group is working together to achieve a result together or play together and 2) for the group to work together to give one or two selected participants an opportunity of doing something or achieving something they would not otherwise do.

Many of the active games involve a smaller number of the group in being very active and the rest providing a framework in which the games can happen.

Some of these games also bring in the competitive element. No matter what you have heard elsewhere there is nothing wrong with competition if it is wisely used in a cooperative atmosphere. In these games, you will be asking for volunteers and it would be quite normal for those who are more competitive to want to be chosen, so it is important to watch out for the more inhibited player and the quieter player and encourage them to volunteer as well.

We tend not to ask for volunteers, but rather ask all the participants to be something and then we will choose one of them. If for example we wanted to select some people to play Russ Off, we may tell the group that we are going to choose from amongst those who do the wildest dance.

More Active Games

As we move into the realms of using masses of energy and going really wild and hyper, we have to watch out because a very active game could become violent and vicious. It is important before moving on to this type of game to stress and constantly reiterate, the safety rules you expect the participants to keep.

It would be sensible to draw attention, if necessary, to the different sizes in people in the group and to make sure that the larger are aware of the smaller, and the smaller aware of the larger and that all participants moderate their own movements so that they do not become a danger to the people they are playing with. It may be a good idea to talk about walking quickly and not running, and to being gentle and not rough.

Ultimate Co-operation

One of the reasons that we get involved in cooperative play is to get a group of people who may have come together just for this occasion, people who are strangers to each other, or individuals, to become part of a group and by working together through the process of play, to learn to work together. What we are aiming at is ultimate co-operation, the time when this group is able and willing to work for the benefit of all.

It is at this time, when the participants have learnt about co-operation that we as the facilitator, can talk about taking some of these skills learnt in the play environment out into the world at large.

That is when we will really experience ultimate co-operation, when it happens and you the play worker or facilitator is not there to make it happen!

Closing Games

It is just as important to finish a session properly as it is to start a session properly. Closing games should enhance what had been happening and help the participants leave whilst they are still glowing.

We should not stop a session by turning to the group and saying, "That's the last game, time to go now" or "We're finished, I was only told to play for an hour". We need to build towards a finish by using phrases like; "...only 15 minutes to go...", "now, before we play the final game", "only enough time for a few more people to try this..."

When finishing a session do not do it in such a way that you are looking for praise from the group. I normally finish with "We're Meynell Games and we'd like to thank you for playing with us and we hope to see you again, Thank you, Good-bye." I have had groups clap and cheer me at the end of a session, and it is great, but it is not something that I set up [at least I try not to!!]

Another Thought

There is also a significant difference between running parachute games at a 'one off' session or when the group of participants have been together for a while as on a playscheme or residential experience.

When the group have been together and already established themselves as a group it is a good time to try some of the more difficult games such as cogs and roll chase.

A Few Words About Meynell Games

Meynell Games is a community based play work organisation committed to developing positive practices in playwork. Meynell Games works towards this by sending small teams of playworkers to provide physical play and creative art play activities at schools, youth clubs and playschemes, by sending larger teams to operate large scale games and various workshops at fetes, festivals, carnivals and other big events.

Meynell Games also provides a range of training services that, like this book, are all based on our own practical playwork experiences.

Meynell Games has a philosophy that guides its approaches in the work it undertakes with children and young people:

The Meynell Games philosophy is not one purely of encouraging participation but is one of never doing anything to discourage participation.

Meynell Games is not an organisation that preaches non competitive play, because we recognise that competition is a fact of life and that young people do not reject competition as long as it is 'fair'. This has led to the Meynell Games approach in which we try to create a cooperative environment in which we may, if people choose to do so, be competitive. This is what we call cooperative competition and is an environment in which all players are equally nurtured, both those who win and those who lose.

We recognise that "children are real people too" and that it is our job as playworkers to nurture and develop that cooperative environment which we must do through our awareness as playworkers (youth workers) of the needs, both individual and group, of the participants.

We believe that activities should not only be about having fun and enjoyment, excitement and challenges, but that they should also provide an opportunity for development and learning.

The Meynell Games philosophy is about being responsive in a positive fashion at all times, and ensuring that the environment is safe and non threatening to allow the participant the opportunity of the discovery of self and others.

This is a book about physical activity. The physical skills that we learn through this play are skills that we learn about responding to other people, listening to other people and being with other people. These are skills that can be taken away from the play environment and used as person to person skills in everyday life — "life is a game and we must all learn to play it".

A Word About Meynell Games Publications

Although Meynell Games Publications was established by Meynell Games it exists as a separate organisational entity. Its primary function is to publish books on practical aspects of playwork, playwork that will normally have been tried out in the Meynell Games environment. It is hoped that in the future books, magazines and articles by other authors will also be published.

Games Sessions Don't Just Happen!

All our activities have to be planned to be effective. You need to consider the beginning, the middle and the end. This could be done by selecting one exercise or more from the introductions, two or three warm up games and then games from any of the other sections. To help you, I've put together some samples of sessions that I have run. All I have done is listed the names of games in the order played.

When putting your programme together there are significant elements that you need to consider: length of session, number playing, age range, ability and previous experience. Write out your list of games and include a couple of back ups.

2 hour outdoor session at a carnival type event, where the participants can come and go as they please

Ripples
Up and Down
Left-Right
Combinations
1 2 3 Up
What's It Like
Colour Change
Mousetrap
Cat and Mouse
Crocodiles
Leaning
Ball off
Russ Off
Trampolining
Egg Toss
Flying High

1 hour session, 30 participants, summer playscheme, 8-11 year olds, first time, indoors.

Start the Play
Waves
Ripples
Up and Down
Left-Right
Combinations
Nicks Game
Crocodiles
Cat and Mouse
Aerobics
Mushroom Walk
Mushroom Fly
Flying High

Start thePlay Game
1st Exercise
Shoe Factory
Waves
Ripples
Up and Down
Left-Right
Nicks Game[extended]
1 2 3 UP
What's It Like[many times]
Colour Change
Mousetrap
Over the Mountain
cat and Mouse
Crocodiles
Sit On It
Pop Corn
Sit On It Version 2
Russ Off

2 HOURS 5-11 YEAR OLDS, 40 PARTICIPANTS, 20 OF THEM HAVE DONE IT BEFORE

Ripples
Up and Down
Left-Right
Combinations
1 2 3 UP
What's It Like
Colour Change
Multi Change Variation
Shoe Factory
Over the Mountain
Leaning
In the Swamp
Aerobics
Cartoon Time
Round in Circles
Turn and Walk
Air Chase
On the Beach
Story Time
Ball Off
Russ Off

THE
GAMES

SECTION 1

INTRODUCTIONS

These are not so much games, more some sensible introductions to the parachute and play. Game number 4 explains how to turn a bucket shaped canopy, [this is one that when held around the rim, is not flat], into a flat canopy.

NAME

START THE PLAY GAME

AGES

Any age.

NUMBERS

Min 10 : Ideal 30 : Max ++

ENERGY LEVEL

Mellow

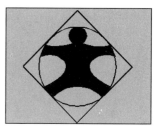

BASIC

Take your parachute out of the bag, explain to the group that it is a real parachute, let them experience it. Remind the group about the fact that as it is a real parachute it has to be treated with care.

SCRIPT

We are going to do some games that some of you have done before. (Hands up) Some of you haven't (Hands up). Wonderful.

Parachute games are a whole new concept. This is a parachute. Who has seen a parachute before? Have any of you touched a parachute before? Some of you haven't. Let me tell you some things about the parachute.

Let me introduce you to the parachute. This is a real parachute. We have it for playing games with as opposed to people having it for jumping out of aeroplanes. It is over 25 years old. When it's over 25 years old it becomes unlawful for it to be used for jumping out of aeroplanes so I can buy them and we can play games with them. Take the parachute, wait for it to come to you, don't move, take the parachute, don't stretch it, stay where you are.

Let me tell you some things about the parachute it's very important that you listen at this time, if you don't understand or if the person next to you doesn't understand try to make sure that they can still join in fully - don't pull it-just leave it where it is.

The parachute is 25 or 26 years old, the date it was made is on it somewhere. It is delicate which means that when we play we have to play carefully. This one has one hole in it already which I shall try to protect whilst we are playing. When we play games with the parachute sometimes we will walk on the parachute and as we move on through the session I will ask you to take your shoes off.

SAFETY

This an introduction, therefore, there are no safety considerations.

MEYNELL SAYS...

This is a good way to start with a small young group, or even a mixed age group - especially indoors. You will have a good calm and controlled start.

OWN NOTES

IF YOU WANT OUR
HELP WE ARE ONLY
A PHONE CALL AWAY
0181 446 5551

FIRST EXERCISE

AGES

Any age.

NUMBERS

Min 10 : Ideal 30 : Max ++

ENERGY LEVEL

Mellow

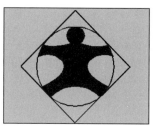

BASIC

With the group sitting on the floor and holding on to the parachute get them to wriggle back. Explain that parachute games are about taking part and whilst there may be competition it does not really matter who wins or who loses.

SCRIPT

There are lots of things we are going to be able to do with the parachute and now we are going to find out what they are.

Everyone hold the parachute and wriggle back with it. Okay you stop here, you lot move back with it. I don't want the parachute pulled tight.

Parachute games make wonderful games, how many of you have played football? How many of you have played netball? How many of you have played any other sort of team games?

How many of you have been on the losing side? Was that nice?

The games that we are going to play, whilst sometimes there are sides, there are never losing sides. This session we are all going to be winners! The reason we are all going to be winners is that some games we're going to play against each other-it doesn't really matter who wins and who loses-and other times we are going to be playing together.

SAFETY

Second introduction with no safety implications.

MEYNELL SAYS...

Still indoors still introducing keeping the group calm.

OWN NOTES

THE SHOE FACTORY

Any age.

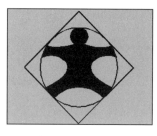

NUMBERS

Min 10 : Ideal 30 : Max ++

ENERGY LEVEL

Calm/Active

BASIC

The object of this game/ exercise is to get people to take their shoes off! Ask them to put one foot in the air and the opposite hand in the air, put their hand on the heel of the foot and separate the shoe from the foot and throw it over the shoulder. Then repeat with other foot!

SCRIPT

Now, everyone sit down...Put your left foot up. Right hand on right heel, remove shoe. Throw. Swap feet and throw...Mega. Shoes are right out of the way yes?

Everyone stand up. Don't shake the parachute. Can we all walk back a little and see what happens. The parachute is wonderful...we can shake it, gently, very gently. We can shake it a little bit harder, and we can go crazy, yeah... and stop. We can also shake the parachute from side to side...this is really difficult, you have to keep your feet still. We move the parachute right and left and right and left....and stop.

We can do other basic movements with the parachute. This one is called down and this one is called up. Want another practice? Down and up. The thing is about the parachute, it's about working together. It's very important that we do things at the same time and together.

In this group we have some people who are this high and we have some people who are this high. Now, what we are going to try to do is that the people who are this high are going to stretch really hard with their hands. Really stretch. The people who are this high, hang on tight. Let's see what happens. Ready...and up.. (screams) and down.

SAFETY

Get the participants to check behind them before throwing their shoes away so that they don't go clobbering anybody with them.

MEYNELL SAYS...

Whilst this is quite fun and exciting, as long as you are careful about the people behind you - remember that in some environments children are always encouraged to undo their laces before pulling their shoes off!!

NAME

MAKING IT FLAT

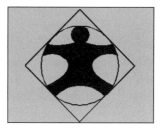

AGES

Suitable for any age, but best with over 8's

BASIC

This is an exercise for parachutes that when held around the perimeter are bucket shaped. Get the group to roll it together towards the middle, stopping it at arbitrarily the first zig zag and making it flat.

NUMBERS

Min 10 : Ideal 20 : Max 40

ENERGY LEVEL

Mellow

SCRIPT

Stand up. This is a reserve parachute. When you jump out of an aeroplane their are two parachutes. Now this one which is 24' in diameter, hopefully, they never open, and there are bigger ones which are flat. We are going to make this one into a flat parachute. Listen carefully, I want everyone to listen to make sure they do it right. This is difficult. We are going to roll the edge of the parachute over nice and tight. We are going to take it up to the first zigzag. So the people who have the points facing away from them are going to have to watch either side. Stop. Make sure you watch the people next to you. Stop. Roll it up a bit more. Stop. Watch the people next to you. Give them some help. Stop. As you can see the parachute has now become flat which means that we can pull it nice and tight. Keep your feet still. Everyone lean back, don't pull back. Just lean back. Because we are doing it together we can stand upright...lean back, stand upright, that is because we are all working together. Stand upright, lean back. Isn't that wonderful?

SAFETY

This is an introduction to bucket shaped parachute canopy's there are no safety implications.

MEYNELL SAYS...

This exercise is only relevant when using a parachute canopy that when held around the rim sags in the middle towards the floor.

OWN NOTES

DRYING THE CHUTE

AGES

Suitable for any age, but the under 6's do have some difficulties with it.

NUMBERS

Min 5 : Ideal 15 : Max 20

ENERGY LEVEL

Active

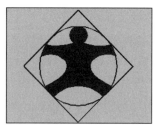

SCRIPT

OK. Everybody run over this side, grab hold of the orange bit with one hand and stand facing away from it. What is going to happen because the parachute is so wet is that you are going to run off into the distance and the parachute is going to fly out behind you in the air and the faster you run the higher it will go a bit like a kite and you will dry it. Instead of you going all the way off, I'm going to watch you disappearing into the distance and then shout out 'pivot!' and the person on the end, your name is, Sarah,; OK. Sarah, when I shout out pivot you stand still as if you were the centre of a circle and everybody else runs round you in a great big arc and then when everyone is straight facing me you will all run back up the field until I shout pivot again, at which point you'll pivot around Sarah and off you go. Grab hold of it and run slowly so everyone has got the idea, and leg it off - there you go - bye! Pivot!

BASIC

This exercise/game will dry a parachute that has been put away wet or played with in a rain storm. The whole group holds on to a small section of the edge of the parachute, holding it over their shoulder facing away from it. One person, at the end of the line, is designated as the pivot. On your instruction the group will run away from you holding the parachute so it flies out behind them. When you shout "pivot" the person designated will stand still and the others will rotate around that person and then they will all run back towards you. This pivoting may be repeated as often as is wished.

SAFETY

Watch out for people tripping over the canopy and for the pivot being pulled over. Tell the participants that if it is to fast, too heavy or that they are not happy with what they are doing to let go.

MEYNELL SAYS...

We learnt this game because we have a belief at Meynell Games that no matter what the weather or what the environment, we should have no excuse not to play.

OWN NOTES

SECTION 2

WARM UPS

These games or exercises should be an integral start to any session. Parachute play is a physical activity and like sport, the participants should warm up before taking part. These exercises not only warm up the appropriate muscles but also the vocal cords.

In addition to their value as warm up exercises, they will also help you learn a little about the group and help with your initial control.

NAME

WAVES

AGES

Any age.

NUMBERS

Min 5 : Ideal 30 : Max ++

ENERGY LEVEL

Calm

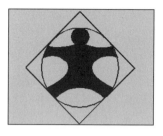

SCRIPT

This is one of the games I specially like. Put the parachute flat on the ground, and look if I just lift up the edge like this, and flap it back down to the ground, you get this wave going underneath. Now if we all do that, we'll get lots of different waves and ripples going under so let's try it OK> you've got to remember to bring the parachute all the way back down to the ground - so your hands come up and then back down to the ground. Don't do it too hard as you'll hurt your knuckles. OK. Try and do it a little more slowly. Maybe just some people from over that side and then some people from over this side and try making different sorts of size waves, big ones or little ones or a whole bunch of little ones all together. Look at those waves - it's like little animals running across underneath. OK> that's brilliant.

BASIC

Lay the parachute on the ground and crouch down next to it. Using small hand movements quickly lift the edge and put it back down on the ground this creates an air bubble that passes underneath. Try different speeds of movement and different heights. You can also try with the whole group or with different sections of the group having a go.

SAFETY

There is a danger that with over enthusiasm the players could knock their knuckles on the ground.

MEYNELL

This game works best on a solid floor, preferably indoors in a gym.

OWN NOTES

NAME

RIPPLES

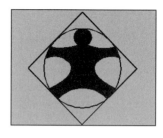

AGES

Any age.

NUMBERS

Min 5 : Ideal 30 : Max ++

ENERGY LEVEL

Calm

BASIC

Everyone stands around the edge of the parachute holding it still and then moving their wrists slowly to make ripples go from the edge to the middle, building up speed and energy, making the ripples go faster and faster and faster.

SCRIPT

OK everybody. Relax and let's start just with our arms bent, elbows digging into our waists and nice and easily start rippling the parachute by shaking your wrists up and down, nice and gently, nice and slowly. get those wrists moving. See the ripples going into the centre of the parachute.

OK Just with the wrists.

Now lets try and speed it up. Get the wrists moving quicker and quicker and faster and faster and faster and faster and...stop.

SAFETY

This is a very safe warm up exercise. There are no additional considerations.

MEYNELL

All Meynell Games sessions tend to start with the same warm up exercises.

OWN NOTES

UP AND DOWN

Any age.

Min 5 : Ideal 30 : Max ++

Active

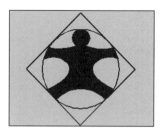

SCRIPT

Hold on to the edge and be still. Now this time we are going to gently move the parachute all the way above our heads and then bring our arms back down. This is a full arm movement, there is no need to bend over. Lets work those arms all the way up and down. Build up a bit of speed and make your arms go faster and faster, quicker and Quicker, till you're going so fast that you've gone totally and completely wild, jumping up and down and stop.

BASIC

The group stands around the edge of the parachute and, using a full arm movement, participants move their arms above their head and down. Try not to bend the body, whilst making large waves go from the edge of the parachute into the middle, building up in speed and energy until everybody is, not only raising their arms up and down, but jumping up and down as well.

SAFETY

This is another safe warm up exercise there are no additional considerations.

MEYNELL

OWN NOTES

LEFT-RIGHT

AGES

Suitable for any age, but the under 6's do have some difficulties with it.

NUMBERS

Min 10 : Ideal 30 : Max ++

ENERGY LEVEL

Calm

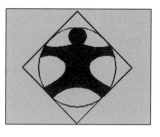

BASIC

The group stand around the edge of the parachute holding it with their arms straight down, hands touching, so, each persons left hand is touching their own right hand. With their feet apart, the group move the parachute from side to side. The object is to get everybody moving in the same direction at the same time and once they have done this to build up speed to as fast as they can go without losing the left right rhythm.

SCRIPT

Stand up. Pull the parachute tight. We are going to move the parachute on a horizontal plane, by that I mean from side to side. OK. lets make the parachute swing sideways. Let's try it.

For this to work, we will have to be swinging the same way at the same time. Let's see if we can manage to work together without having to call out left, right, left, right, (if the group can not work together call out "left right left right").

This is really difficult but we will get there.

SAFETY

Ensure that the participants arms remain straight. If they bend their arms, not only do they end up pulling the canopy from side to side, but are in danger of hitting the person next to them with their elbows. This is of great concern if there are large people standing next to small people as then their elbows are likely to hit them in the head.

MEYNELL

It's energetic, it's fun, it's confusing - but watch out for the sore fingertips and the aching arms.

OWN NOTES

NAME

COMBINATIONS

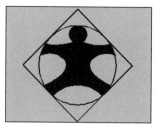

AGES

Suitable for any ages, but the under 5's tend just to shake it around.

NUMBERS

Min 10 : Ideal 30 : Max ++

ENERGY LEVEL

Wild

BASIC

The group stands around the edge of the parachute holding on to the edge and following instructions move the parachute in specified directions; e.g. left-up, right-up or left-right-up-down. They start slowly and build up to as fast as they can go.

SCRIPT

Alright, so we've tried going left to right. We've tried going up and down quickly and we've tried going up and down slowly and now it's time to see if we can put all of those things together. So standing with you feet a little bit a part, holding on to the parachute, be relaxed, move your hands to the left, left and then up and then right, and then down, you should be back where you started, having gone round in one big circle.

Alright let's do it. Call it out with me. Left. Up. Right. Down. Faster. Left, up, right, down. Left, up, right, down. Left, up, right, down, left, up, right, down, left, up, right, down, left up, right, down. Excellent. Now let's try going the other way. Right. Up. Left. Down. Right, up, left, down, right, up, left, down, faster, faster, call it out louder, together, GO!

SAFETY

Make sure that this does not become too energetic/rough, because if it does it can alienate smaller participants and possibly cause them to get pulled around.

MEYNELL

OWN NOTES

NAME

NICK'S GAME

AGES

Any age.

NUMBERS

Min 5 : Ideal 30 : Max ++

ENERGY LEVEL

Wild

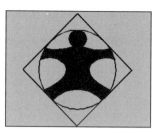

SCRIPT

This is another game that is quite fun and , well let's try it. Put the parachute to your toes, to your nose, your knees, shoulders, head, toes, nose, shoulders, knees, nose, head (progressively said more quickly!), toes, shoulders, shoulders, toes, confused you, toes, knees, toes, knees, toes, shoulders, head. Very confusing, very fast, excellent; let's move on.

BASIC

The group hold the parachute and on the instructions of knees, toes, shoulders, head, hold it at the appropriate point on the body. This is a warm up game and so the movements should be varied between fast and slow.

SAFETY

When this really gets going it can be very fast — so be careful of shoulder joints!

MEYNELL

There I was out at a session one day letting my team of staff get on with the job, when I heard all this giggling, laughter and energy. I turned round to discover that Nick had invented his own warm up. Hence this is called Nick's Game and no matter what, I can never run this one as well as he can!

OWN NOTES

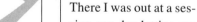

AGES

Suitable for any age

NUMBERS

Min 10 : Ideal 30 : Max ++

ENERGY LEVEL

Active

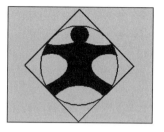

SCRIPT

OK everybody crouch down to the ground. Keep your knees off the ground and your bottom off the ground, knees bent, back straight, holding on to the parachute. Now what's going to happen is, I'm going to count, one, two, three, UP and on the word UP, I want everybody to stand up, holding on to the edge of the parachute and stretch their hands high into the air like this.

OK everybody ready? Keep your back straight, knees bent, bottoms off the ground, everybody holding on and one, two three, UP. Excellent, straight back down to the ground. Try to keep your feet still when we do this. Let's do it again. Everybody ready. Knees off the ground, bottom off the ground and one,, two three, UP. Excellent. Back down to the ground. Take a little bunny hop backwards to pull the canopy flat on the ground and one, two, three, UP.

BASIC

The parachute is placed on the floor and the group crouch around the outside of the parachute knees off the ground, bottoms off the ground. Following the instructions One, Two, Three, on the word UP, everybody stands up together and stretches their hands as high above their heads as they can.

SAFETY

When performing this exercise in a dusty or hard surface area suggest to the participants that as they stand up and raise their hands above their heads that they close their eyes, because any dust or loose bits on the ground will be pulled up with the parachute.

MEYNELL

OWN NOTES

NAME

WHAT'S IT LIKE

AGES

Suitable for any age, but better with older groups.

NUMBERS

Min 10 : Ideal 30 : Max ++

ENERGY LEVEL

Calm

SAFETY

The same considerations as One. Two Three, UP, otherwise this is a simple, safe exercise.

BASIC

The group perform a One, Two, Three, UP and then whilst it is UP using their imagination they look at the shape it makes. Once they bring it back to the ground their shapes are called out and imagination is encouraged (it is traditionally called a mushroom, so imagination needs to work a lot harder than that).

SCRIPT

OK. This time when the parachute goes up into the air I want you to have a look at the shape that it makes, because it could look like something, depending on what sort of imagination you have. I'd like you to look at the shape it makes and to be as wild and as wacky and as imaginative, as stupid as you want and put your hand up when it comes back down to the ground and I'll come round and get your thoughts on what it looks like.

Everybody down to the ground, knees off the ground, bottoms off the ground, back straight, one, two, three, UP. Look at the shape what does it look like? Use your imagination, be creative, don't put your hand up now, I want you to come OK down to the ground, hands up if you have got an idea, I'm coming round.

Parachute. Yes we know that it looks like a parachute. Circus Top, Spiders Web, Umbrella, Mushroom, Circle, Balloon, Jellyfish, Igloo, Cloud.

OK Let's do that one more time and see if we can come up with anymore strange, wild and crazily, stupidly wonderful ideas. Down to the ground, One, Two, Three, UP.

Parachute, we've had parachute. Let's try to make sure that you call out things that haven't been called already. Ostrich, Someone's belly, Triangle, OK the wilder the crazier the ideas I don't mind. Ice Cream, Apple. OK Excellent. Great, Super. Thank you very much. Now instead of going one, Two, Three UP, because saying UP is very boring we are going to go one, two, three and say Igloo, that's one of the suggestions we had so we'll use Igloo and everybody shouts out Igloo as you stand up. Let's try it, One, Two, Three, (everybody shout) IGLOO. Excellent and back down to the ground.

MEYNELL

If anyone says it looks like a parachute — shoot them!!

OWN NOTES

IF YOU WANT OUR HELP WE ARE ONLY A PHONE CALL AWAY
0181 446 5551

SECTION 3

CLASSIC GAMES

This next section includes most of the games that you who have played with a parachute before will know. I have called them 'Classic games' but in some ways you will see from the script that the Meynell Games way of running them may be different from your own experience.

The biggest problem with 'Classic Games' is that because we have played them so often we can tend to get bored with them. So some of these games appear in the book in other guises!!

NAME

MUSHROOM WALK

AGES

Suitable for any age, but the under 6's do have some difficulties with it.

NUMBERS

Min 15 : Ideal 30 : Max ++

ENERGY LEVEL

Active

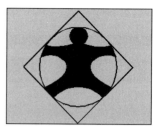

BASIC

The group performs as in Mushroom, but as soon as they have called out mushroom they walk towards the centre of the circle. The parachute will rise higher and if the group have all walked together at the same speed, the apex will fall back down in the middle of the group.

SCRIPT

Everyone stand up. Hold the parachute. What we are going to do in this game is we are all going down to the ground, holding the parachute and when I count 1 2 3 UP we are all going to stand up together and stretch our hands as far above our heads as we can. OK. Let's try it.

OK. Now remember doing the One, Two, Three, UP. Now this time as soon as we go up we're going to walk in towards the centre of the parachute, the parachute will be in the air. So we're just going to walk in, now if we walk in gently and calmly together, well, let's do it and see what happens. Everybody down to the ground, knees off the ground, bottom off the ground. One, two, three, IGLOO and walk together, no together, together, some people are walking much too quickly. Alright, everyone back out. Careful, don't tread on the canopy and crouch down to the ground. As you will have seen, what happens is, the parachute gets higher and higher in the air and if we all walk in at the same speed the middle of the parachute, which is called the apex, will fall back down in the centre of the circle. If any one part of the circle walks in much quicker than another part, it will fall down over the back of your heads. Except if it is very windy or there is a gust of wind it will just go in that direction anyway.

So let's try it. Down to the ground, I'll go one, Two, Three, you shout out IGLOO, I say walk, we all walk in together. One, Two, Three, (everybody shouts) IGLOO! Walk. That's it good, walk in together, not too fast, not too fast. Gently, gently, Oh almost into the middle. Excellent!

SAFETY

A simple exercise, except if there is a group of participants who run towards the middle.

MEYNELL

Don't do what I often do in this game. I keep forgetting to tell the group to hold on to the parachute when they walk forward. However you could play a variation in which after you have walked forward you then let go, grab hold of the opposite edge and walk straight out again.

OWN NOTES

MUSHROOM FLY

AGES

Suitable for any age, but the under 6's do have some difficulties with it.

NUMBERS

Min 15 : Ideal 30 : Max +

ENERGY LEVEL

Mellow

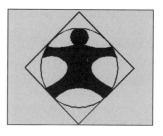

BASIC

Perform as for Mushroom, but as soon as the arms have gone into the air, everybody lets go of the parachute canopy and it will float upwards in a flat circle, if everybody lets go at the same time.

SCRIPT

Alright, what we are going to do now, and this doesn't always work too well outdoors, but we are going to try it, we are going to try if we can make the actual parachute itself fly. You saw how high it could get when we did a walk. Now when we do a fly, it should be able to get higher, and what we do is, we do our one, two, three IGLOO, and then we throw our hands into the air and at the same time we must all let go.

Well let's try it and see what happens. One, two, three, IGLOO, and let go. OK, well what happened there is that we didn't all let go at the same time. So grab hold of it again, pick it up, careful not to tread on it or anybody else and bring it back down to the ground, bunny hop backwards, pull it tight, knees off the ground, bottom off the ground. Alright, I'll try to help, so what I'll do, I'll count one two three, you all shout out IGLOO and then I'll say FLY. Everybody let's go on the word FLY. One, two, three, IGLOO, FLY! Excellent and it takes off like a flying saucer up into the air. That's brilliant. Now if we were indoors, we would get it sticking to the ceiling. OK let's do that a couple more times and see if we can get to go even higher and stay as a circle for longer.

SAFETY

A simple and safe exercise as long as you remember to close your eyes when you lift it up off a dusty floor.

MEYNELL

I do like this idea and once in every 50 goes you might get it to work spinning of in a perfect circle.

OWN NOTES

NAME

COLOUR CHANGE

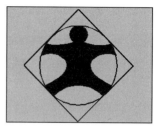

AGES

Any age.

NUMBERS

Min 10 : Ideal 30 : Max +

ENERGY LEVEL

Active

BASIC

The group do a mushroom but as soon as they have called out Mushroom, one person calls out a colour and anybody wearing that colour lets go of the edge of the parachute and crosses places by going underneath and coming out again at the other side.

SCRIPT

Everyone stand up. Hold the parachute. What we are going to do in this game is we are all going down to the ground, holding the parachute and when I count 1 2 3 UP we are all going to stand up together and stretch our hands as far above our heads as we can.

OK let's try it. Everyone down, 1 2 3 UP! OK Let's go down again, this time try to up on the up. Not on the three and not after the up. We all have to do it together... 1 2 3 UP!

Let's go down again, when we go up, try to keep your back straight. Bend your knees, keep your back straight. We don't want any injuries and if we don't lift properly we could strain our backs.

This time, as we go up, I am going to call out a colour and if you are wearing that colour, whether we can see it or not, let go of the parachute, go underneath and find a space on the opposite side and hold on again. You have to move quickly, but don't run, because we don't want anyone to run into anyone else and we don't want the big people knocking over the little people.

Everyone down. Everyone ready...1 2 3 UP Magenta (repeat as often as you like using what colour you like).

Try using foods people like, length of hair, or any other category you can think of). If the group is working well, try calling out first two colours and then build to lots of colours, see if you can eventually get everyone to change place at the same time.

SAFETY

The big danger here is of people running into each other underneath. Try starting the game with people walking and then speed it up once people know what's going to happen. Keep reminding them about the danger of running into or being run into.

MEYNELL

Everybody cheats in this game — so what!! The emphasis is about participating and it really doesn't matter so long as people are enjoying themselves and not wrecking the game!

OWN NOTES

IF YOU WANT OUR HELP WE ARE ONLY A PHONE CALL AWAY 0181 446 5551

MULTI CHANGE VARIATION

AGES

Any age.

NUMBERS

Min 8 : Ideal 30 : Max ++

ENERGY LEVEL

Active

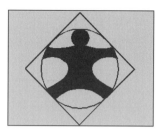

SCRIPT

Now this time instead of calling out a colour or a category I'm going to give you each a number. 1, 2, 3, 4, 1, 2, 3, 4, 1, 2, 3, 4, 1, 2, 3, 4, 1, 2, 3, 4, 1, 2, 3, 4, 1, 2, 3, 4, 1, 2 OK try to remember your number. Now get ready, remember I'll count 1, 2, 3, UP and on the up you stand up and holding the parachute stretch as high as you can go. As soon as you go up I will call out a number and the people with that number go underneath and come out into a space on another side. You got that? OK 1, 2, 3, up, number 2 quickly, go change places, again, down to the ground, 1, 2, 3, up numbers 1 and 3, down to the ground ready to go, 1, 2, 3, up, 1, 3, and 4,

Excellent, again, I hope you're ready for this! 1, 2, 3, up, 1, 2, 3, 4,. OK pick the parachute back up and let's do something else.

BASIC

Give a person in the group a number, 1, 2, 3, 4, by going round the edge of the canopy and numbering each person making sure they know which number they are. Remind them how to do the 1, 2, 3, Up movement, as they go up you call out a number and the people with that number will change place by going under the canopy. Start with one number and build. If you are really brave try all four!!

SAFETY

Same considerations as colour change.

MEYNELL

Doing it this way becomes more controlled. it doesn't stop the cheating but then again who cares!

OWN NOTES

CAT & MOUSE

AGES

Suitable for any age

NUMBERS

Min 8 : Ideal 30 : Max ++

ENERGY LEVEL

Hyper/Wild

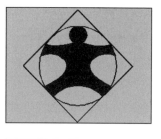

SCRIPT

Alright I want everyone to sit down round the side of the parachute. Can I have two volunteers? OK the first volunteer come on top of the parachute, you are going to be a mouse. Show me how a mouse moves. OK> that's good but has anyone else seen a two legged mouse before. Now try being a mouse on all fours. Get as small as you can, remember, mice are very small creatures. You want to try making a mouse noise.

OK., the other volunteer, you are a cat. Let's do a quick cat impersonation.

The object of the game is for the cat to catch the mouse.. BUT ..the mouse is under the parachute, and the cat is on the top. OK. mouse, under you go.

Now...when we are playing we can either help the mouse by shaking the parachute (shake viciously) or help the cat by holding the parachute tight on to the ground (do so). See, there is the mouse. Let's start with the mouse and the cat on opposite sides of the parachute and you two remember you must go in a clockwise direction and cat no going over the centre part.

Let's go!

when the cat has caught the mouse, get two new volunteers to play the roles. How about Siamese cats and Siamese mice? Think about putting a dog in the game as well).

BASIC

The parachute is flat on the ground, with the group standing or sitting or crouching around the outside. One person selected to be the cat, who go on top of the parachute as a cat. Another person is selected to be a mouse, who goes underneath the parachute. The cat has to catch the mouse. The group around the outside aid the mouse by shaking the parachute very vigorously or aid the cat by holding the parachute flat on the ground.

SAFETY

This can be quite painful on the knees. Working on an extremely hard surface suggests that they adopt a non knee on the ground approach. The second thing to watch out for is that the cat does not splat the mouse.

MEYNELL

If you are an experienced parachute player you will have played this zillions of times and be totally bored by it. Be brave - skip this page and go straight to Cartoon Time!

OWN NOTES

CROCODILES

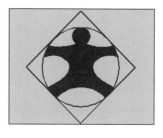

AGES

Any age.

NUMBERS

Min 10 : Ideal 30 : Max ++

ENERGY LEVEL

Hyper/Wild

BASIC

The group sit around the side of the parachute with their legs underneath and the parachute pulled up tight to their tummies. One person is selected to be a crocodile. The crocodile goes underneath the parachute and slithers around biting at peoples legs. A person, when bitten, gives a loud blood curdling scream and then goes underneath the parachute to become an additional crocodile. Those who are not crocodiles will shake the parachute to make it into a swamp.

SCRIPT

I'd like a volunteer who is going to be a crocodile so may I please see a volunteering crocodile. I want to see a crocodile. Excellent. OK I have a crocodile, what's your name crocodile. John OK. you're coming on top and I'd like you to lie down in the middle of the canopy, on your front. Excellent and show everybody your crocodile. Now what are you going to use a s your crocodiles mouth. Excellent using your arms, massive great big snout, big chomping jaws. OK Croc John, It's tea time and you are a very hungry crocodile. Now, what's going to happen in this game is we're all going to sit around the parachute and we're going to magically change the parachute into a swamp by rippling it. Good. We're going to stick our feet in the swamp, by putting our legs under the canopy. We must be a bunch of very stupid human beings because here we are dangling our legs in the swamp and it's tea time and there's bound to be a hungry crocodile. If there's a hungry crocodile, the crocodile is going to eat our feet isn't it? Yes. So Croc John in a minute will go underneath and start crocking around underneath the canopy until he finds a nice healthy pair of legs which he will give an enormous, massive great big chomp at. OK, and when you get chomped, what happens to you? Yes, yes you scream that's right. OK. on the count of three I'd like everyone to demonstrate their most blood curdling scream. One, two, three Ahhhhhhhhh!

Brilliant, and as soon as you scream you die and go into the swamp and become another crocodile crocking around on your belly. Are you ready? OK Croc John under you go, let's ripple the parachute to make the swamp and of course remember everybody if you don't want to go underneath, you don't have to so don't worry and Croc John off you go.

SAFETY

Remind participants to slide or crawl around underneath the canopy, not to walk as they may end up treading on people.

MEYNELL

If you are an experienced parachute player you will have played this zillions of times and be totally bored by it. Be brave - skip this page and go straight to In the Swamp

OWN NOTES

NAME

SHARKS

AGES

Any age.

NUMBERS

Min 10 : Ideal 30 : Max ++

ENERGY LEVEL

Active/Hyper

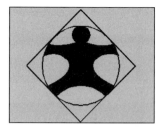

BASIC

The group stand around the edge of the canopy with it pulled fairly tight. One person is selected to be the shark. They go underneath the canopy and make a fin with their hands. The fin sticks up through the canopy. The shark runs around underneath, the fin cutting through the parachute until they decide to suddenly dart for one person at the side. They grab that person and swap positions. The new shark continues.

SCRIPT

Let's have everybody standing up around the edge of the parachute and take one step back a bit, pull it tight, but don't pull it over Wonderful! I'd like a volunteer shark. Who's going to be my shark for me. OK, now you're a standing up sort of shark what are you going to use a shark fin? Hand on the head with the fingers pointing upwards Excellent! OK shark what's your name, OK Zenovia, Zenovia the Shark. Under you go, now you're going to shark around underneath with your fin up tight against the edge of the parachute canopy so that everybody around the outside can see this fin and you're going to hover around underneath and you're going to go towards the edge and then back towards the centre and at some point you are going to fly right towards the edge grab one person by the waist and they will swap places and go under the parachute instead as you. OK off you go, don't go straight to the edge, zig zag around, get everyone at the side scared, OK who knows the jaws theme, let's hum it. Here comes that shark, here comes that shark, and they grab someone and swap places and the next shark off you go.

SAFETY

A basically simple game but there is a possibility for the sharks fins to catch on the bands and strings of the canopy and they need to be warned about this.

MEYNELL

I have played this game so many times and I am never failed to be amazed by that fact the when the shark is coming for you everyone seems to jump or scream when the shark comes straight at them.

OWN NOTES

NAME

FLYING HIGH (VERSION 2)

AGES

Suitable for any age, but better with older groups.

NUMBERS

Min 10 : Ideal 30 : Max ++

ENERGY LEVEL

Active

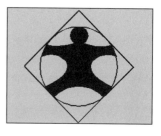

BASIC

Teach the group how to lift the parachute, either by leaning or mushrooming. Then select a volunteer who sits in the middle. The group then lifts the parachute and gently lowers it.

SCRIPT

OK. who is very little and very brave? Are you very brave? What's your name? (very gentle voice) OK. Debra we are going to make you fly. Debra is going to have a flying lesson. Obviously we have to remember that our passenger is a human being and therefore very delicate and we do not want any harm to come to Debra do we.....(Noooo). So listen carefully.

We are going to stand and make sure the parachute is pulled tight. We are going to make Debra fly. We are going to go down, wait and then we are going to go up and then we don't go down again, we hold it in this position. Down.... we are not going to throw her. Debra have you got a nice solid head? If we throw you to the ceiling will you be alright? OK. everyone down. And...up! And down!

It would be lovely for everyone to have a go. Unfortunately we do not have time for that. I would like the people who have done it before not to volunteer until others who have not had a chance before have had an opportunity. Who has not done it before? If you have not done it before keep your hands up. Down and up and down... (repeat).

SAFETY

It is very important to make sure that the group is going to be responsible enough so that once the person has gone up into the air they are lowered gently to the ground. If possible put cushions or a mat under the person in the middle so that if they do come down hard they don't hit the ground.

MEYNELL

OWN NOTES

NAME

THE WAVE

AGES

Suitable for any age, but the under 6's do have some difficulties with it.

NUMBERS

Min 15 : Ideal 30 : Max ++

ENERGY LEVEL

Active

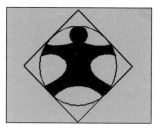

BASIC

The group stand around the side of the parachute. The objective is to make like a Mexican wave travelling around the edge. One person starts. They stretch above their heads with the parachute then back down to the ground. As soon as the person on their right feels themselves being pulled up they go up and continue the movement. Thus, the movement continues around the edge of the parachute canopy.

SCRIPT

OK does everybody know how to do a Mexican Wave? Some do, some don't. OK this is what we do, drop the parachute on the ground, I lift my hands up into the air and put them down again and as soon as my hands start going down, the person on my left, their hands go up and down andas soon as their hands go down the person on their left...you got it OK. Let's try that, I'll start up, OK keep it going wait for the persons arms to go down and all the way round. OK. Let's see if we can do that again, only a little bit faster. Excellent!

We'll now try that but actually holding on to the parachute at the same time. So you're going to feel your hands being pulled up and pulled down, go with the flow and try not to race ahead of the canopy. I'll start and here we go, wait for it to come to you, and back to me. Excellent. Now we'll do that again and see if we can make it go even faster. Brilliant!

Everyone stand up and hold the parachute at waist level. What we are going to do is make a wave travel around the outside of the parachute. It is hard, very hard, but we are going to try. Any suggestions as to how we are going to do it? (Discussion, try). We have to do it one after the other, you don't do it until the person on your right has done it. Let's try it. OK. Go on. Well that was close but it died. (Move people around big ones next to little ones). Try it again. Watch the person on your right and wait for it...getting better....Lets try another method because it died again.

Let's try this. Everyone know their left hand from their right hand? Left hands...right hands...What I am going to do is I am going to push the parachute down with my right hand, what does that do to Sharon's right hand?

SAFETY

This is a simple and safe exercise but when it does build up in speed, there is a potential for your arms to get stretched a touch.

MEYNELL

OWN NOTES

NAME

THE WAVE (VERSION 2)

AGES

Suitable for mixed age groups but not for the very young ones

NUMBERS

Min 10 : Ideal 30 : Max ++

ENERGY LEVEL

Active

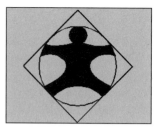

SCRIPT

If I put my right hand down on the ground, the person standing on my right...Sharon...should find your left hand being pulled down towards the ground and then, your right hand will follow your left hand down towards the ground and the person next to you will follow...left hand...and right hand...In the meantime, my right hand will have gone back up into the air, pulling your left hand up, followed by your right, etc. etc. etc.

Let's try it. Ah.. you have got to wait until your hand is pulled down before you go down. Wait for the wave to come to you, don't jump ahead of it. Let's really try and make this wave spin round this circle.

This is good, now let's try it and really stretch our arms up and down. This gives us a bigger wave. That was very good. At last we are working together.

BASIC

Explain to the group that you wish to make a wave travel around the parachute. Ask for ideas on how to do it. Try some of the ideas. If they do not work suggest to the group that they see what happens if you pull your left hand down towards the ground, what happens to the persons right hand next to you and yes that one follows. So to make the wave the starting person pulls their left hand down then the person next to them will pull their right hand down followed by the left and so on round the circle.

SAFETY

A simple exercise with no safety implications.

MEYNELL

OWN NOTES

ROUND IN CIRCLES

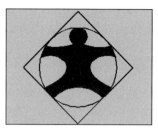

AGES

Any age.

NUMBERS

Min 10 : Ideal 30 : Max ++

ENERGY LEVEL

Active

BASIC

The group stands up holding on to the parachute in one hand, all the players using the same hand, with the other hand stretched away from the parachute so they are standing sideways to the canopy. The object is to walk in a circle turning the parachute and keeping the apex [the centre] where it is. Once the group is walking effectively, speed it up by getting them to walk faster, jog, run, and finally sprinting. It is important that you slow it down by reversing the order, sprint, run, jog, walk.

SCRIPT

Everyone stand up. Hold the parachute with your left hand and pull it until it's tight.

This is not a tug of war, we are not trying to pull people over on the other side. We are just trying to pull it tight.

Imagine it is a sheet of steel. See where the middle is? We are going to try and keep the middle exactly where it is and we are going to walk turning the parachute. Then have the parachute in our left hand, all facing the same direction...let's start walking.

We have got to keep the middle where it is. It means thinking about what you are doing and trying to make sure we are all pulling at the same strength, that's good we have got it going nice and slowly. Let's try to walk a bit quicker, and a bit quicker. Let's start jogging. This is great. Let's jog a bit faster. Let's run, brilliant. Let's sprint, run as fast as we can.

Now, a little bit slower. Don't stop, keep running, slow it down to a jog, a bit slower, let's slow it down to a walk, lets walk slower, let's stop.

SAFETY

Warn people that if it gets too fast for them to let go and get out of the way. When slowing it down make sure that it is a progression and that you don't just stop. If you just stop people will run into each other, that's when they can get hurt.

MEYNELL

OWN NOTES

ON THE BEACH

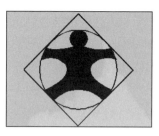

AGES

Any age.

NUMBERS

Min 2 : Ideal 30 : Max 40

ENERGY LEVEL

Mellow/Wild

SCRIPT

OK I'd like you all to come and sit in this section over here. Sit, really squeeze up close to each other and get sitting on the edge and very, very close to each other. Now, imagine you are sitting on the beach and waves are gently rippling in towards you. Imagine the sun disappearing behind thick dark clouds and the waves getting stronger and stronger and stronger and heavier and faster and the rain lashing down, suddenly an almighty, massive, enormous great big wave comes flying and crashes over you. OK. Let's do this again and this time as the wave gets bigger and bigger and heavier, you can choose to dive forwards into it, just remember that the ground is underneath and if you dive too soon the wave is just going to let you through and you'll crash into the ground.

BASIC

All but two of the group sit on the edge of the parachute canopy as close together as they can get. The remaining two stand at 4 o'clock and 8 o'clock to the group shaking the parachute gently as a wave until it is a big enough to go crashing over the top of those who are sitting.

SAFETY

This is initially a simple and safe exercise, however, when the participants decide to dive into the wave make sure that they know they will end up on the ground and on each other.

MEYNELL

Why is it that Karen seems to get this game to work better than I do?

OWN NOTES

POPCORN

AGES

Good for all ages

NUMBERS

Min 4 : Ideal 30 : Max ++

ENERGY LEVEL

Calm/Wild

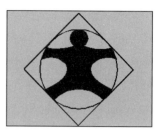

BASIC

With the group standing up and holding the edge of the parachute put one ball in the middle and make it bounce around, then add many more balls. Size 4 or size 5 balls are ideal. The group can shake with any level of energy trying to make the balls pop like popcorn into the air.

SCRIPT

Holding on to the edge of the parachute, let's just make it ripple, shake it around, a little bit of energy there, wonderful. Let's throw on one ball,. Make it bounce. Work at it together, hard or slow as you like, that's good. Now, a whole bag of balls - we call this game pop corn and let's pop that corn! Try to keep the balls on, just popping them high. Let's see how high we can make the pop corn jump. One at a time, two at a time, excellent. Lots of pop corn bouncing up and down there, wonderful.

SAFETY

Watch out for balls flying off, and into your face.

MEYNELL

OWN NOTES

IF YOU WANT OUR
HELP WE ARE ONLY
A PHONE CALL AWAY
0181 446 5551

TRAINING

If we do it . . .
We offer training in it!

Call for current
details and prices

10 Grove Road,
London N12 9DY
0181 446 5551

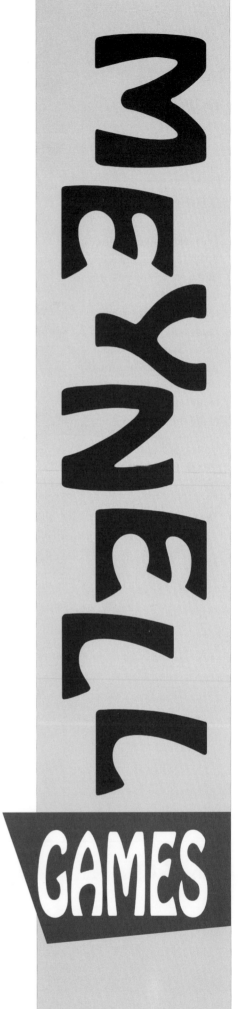

SECTION 4

CHASE GAMES

Meynell Games has never preached non competitive play, in fact we believe there can be value to competition. However what we must remember is that when we use competition, it is there to enhance each participant's experience. We aim to create a cooperative environment in which we can be as competitive as we like. This means that the outcome of the competition is unimportant although the process can send the adrenaline shooting through the veins!

MUTANTS

NUMBERS

Min 8 : Ideal 30 : Max ++

ENERGY LEVEL

Hyper/Wild

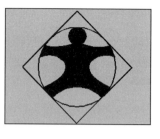

BASIC

The group stand around the edge of the parachute and throw the edge forwards. Each person stands so that they are just on the parachute. One person is selected to be a mutant and after making their mutant type movements they are then sent underneath the parachute. They "mute" around until they are near an edge where they lean down, put one hand out from the edge and grab the ankle of someone standing on the outside who then becomes a mutant and goes underneath with them.

SCRIPT

We are going to play mutants. Everyone stand up. Let go of the parachute. Get your shoes off. Push the parachute in a bit so it is loose and stand with both feet on the edge of the parachute.

Who watches science fiction and horror movies. Oh, at least there are some of you. You have all seen a mutant then. OK. who is going to be our mutant? OK. you go under the parachute. Alright, I want you to be the most horrible, grotesque, noisy, scary mutant you can be. BRILLIANT.

The mutant is going to mute around under the parachute and suddenly a hand will come out of the side of the parachute and grab your leg and when that happens you go underneath the parachute as well and you can be any sort of mutant you want. We will end up with masses of mutants muting around underneath.

Whilst you are standing on the outside of the parachute you have to keep your feet still. Any questions? Let's go.

SAFETY

Check for claustrophobia under the canopy and watch out for people treading on each other.

MEYNELL

I am not sure whether calling this game "Mutants" is politically correct, but when Peter invented it at Redbourne in 1988 he called it mutants — and the name has stuck!

OWN NOTES

IN THE SWAMP

Good for all ages

Min 8 : Ideal 30 : Max ++

Active/Wild

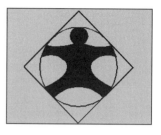

SCRIPT

In this game we are going to magically transform the parachute into a swamp and we do it like this. We sit down, we stick our legs underneath and we wriggle backwards. We then ripple the parachute, and it magically turns from a parachute into a boggy, smelly swamp, and for this game I will be needing someone to put themselves forward to be a swamp creature. What sort of swamp creatures do we have? OK> What sort of swamp creature are you? You're a frog so we are going to have a frog in our swamp today. OK show me your frog ribbet, thank you very much. Now, your name frog is ANGUS, Angus the frog. OK Angus the frog, you are going to go into the swamp and frog up and down, ribbet around, and as soon as you feel like it you will pounce on a pair of the legs at the side , you'll grab hold of them and they will be dragged screaming and dying into the swamp where they transform and become yet another frog and we shall end up with a whole swamp full of frogs ribbeting around. Let's go frog!

BASIC

The group sit with their legs under the parachute. You explain to them that you are going to turn the parachute into a swamp by making ripples and ask them to put forward ideas of swamp creatures. Get the participants to demonstrate how their creatures move and what noises it makes. Then select one person to go under the canopy into the swamp. They will go around underneath acting like their creatures catching people on the outside who then go under the canopy into the swamp until all who have gone into the swamp want to go and the swamp is full of creatures.

SAFETY

Same safety as crocodiles. Remember to finish the game before everyone has gone underneath — those last players might be the ones or are scared or unsure and don't want to go.

MEYNELL

This is a great variation on Crocodiles for playing when the ground is wet, hard or generally unpleasant.

Remember — you are playing it this way because you are fed up with Crocodiles, so encourage the group to use their imagination when thinking of swamp creatures.

OWN NOTES

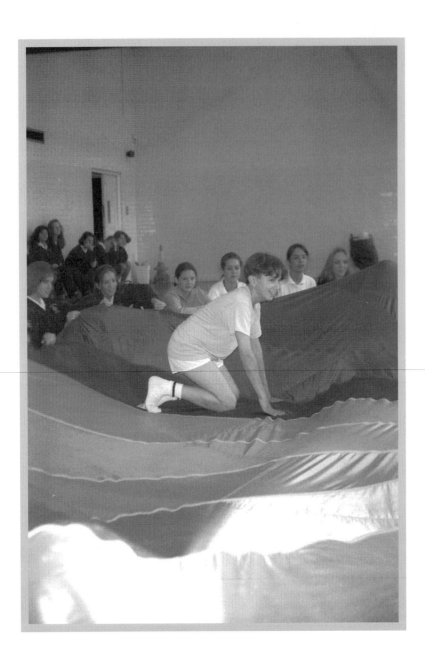

AGES

Good for all ages

NUMBERS

Min 6 : Ideal 30 : Max ++

ENERGY LEVEL

Active/Wild

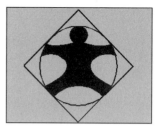

BASIC

Explain to the group that this is a game based on cartoon characters and ask for some ideas. Choose one of the characters and find out who chases them or who they chase and find out who their opponent is. Select one person to be the cartoon character and someone to be its opponent and play a game of chase with one person underneath and one on top. It does not matter which one is on top or underneath.

SCRIPT

Everybody crouch around the side in this game I would like two cartoon characters or any cartoon characters. It is a game of chase and one cartoon character, as they so often do, chases and tries to eat, kill, squash, splatter or blat the other one, so who shall we have? Road runner, OK show me your road runner. Thank you, and your name is , Piers, OK Piers road runner who are you chasing? coyote, thank you very much, and who is going to be coyote? You are! Coyote you'll be underneath, being chased by road runner. I don't really watch this one so I don't know what happens but let's take it from here! Everybody can stand up and can shake the parachute or do whatever you like to make life easier or hard for road runner and coyote. Off you go! Oh, caught very quickly; move over here road runner and carry on! Brilliant, wonderful, wonderful and let's have a count down from 10 10 9 8 7 6 5 4 3 2 1 OK road runner off, thank you very much, Coyote out thank you very much, another two cartoon characters please!

SAFETY

Same as cat an mouse.

MEYNELL

You don't need to be in touch with TV> — use the children's knowledge and imagination.

OWN NOTES

SIAMESE CAT AND MOUSE

AGES

Any age.

NUMBERS

Min 8 : Ideal 30 : Max ++

ENERGY LEVEL

Active

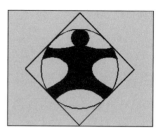

BASIC

Almost identical to cat and mouse except that in this version two people become one cat and two people become one mouse. The two people are permanently joined together for the game like Siamese twins - joined at birth

SCRIPT

We've played cat and mouse and now it's time for a bit of a variation, so this time instead of having one cat and one mouse, we shall have Siamese cats and you know what a Siamese cat is? Yep, a Siamese cat is two people joined together, joined at birth. And two Siamese mice to be chased. Now remember, joined at birth, do not let go of each other> Siamese cats on top, thank you, Siamese mice underneath. Everybody else strand up and you can either help the cats or help the mice and off we go!

SAFETY

Ensure that the pairs don't pull each other around.

MEYNELL

OWN NOTES

IF YOU WANT OUR
HELP WE ARE ONLY
A PHONE CALL AWAY
0181 446 5551

AIR CHASE

AGES

7-8 upwards

NUMBERS

Min 15 : Ideal 30 : Max ++

ENERGY LEVEL

Calm/Active

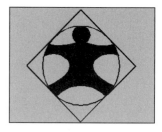

SCRIPT

In this game I am going to ask for two people to put themselves forward and they are going to be playing chase with a difference. Let us demonstrate! Everybody hold onto the parachute with both hands and lean backwards. What happens is the parachute goes tight and comes off the ground, to about our waist level, like that, excellent. We shall take one chosen person who shall go on top of the parachute. Let the parachute down, let them go on top, and lean back again. OK start near the middle, just run round. Now when you are near the middle it comes down and hits the ground but if you walk out to the edge, and keep walking around the side, you'll find there you are up in the air. Hold it still there and let's get a second person on opposite. Walk around, feel comfortable, and now you can start chasing after each other as fast as you like! The object here is to remain as close to the outside as you can, moving round quickly so that no one person has to hold your weight. And chase! Cheated across the middle there but never mind, caught and down to the ground and let's choose two more people.

BASIC

Make sure that the group is able to lean backwards whilst holding on to the parachute and stretch it so that it is tight. When they can do this select one person to stand on top and walk around. If the group is able to manage to keep them off the ground most of the time then select a second person and starting them on opposite sides of the parachute, whilst the group keeps them in the air they play chase. Remind the runners on the parachute that the further they are from the centre of the parachute the easier it is for them to stay in the air.

SAFETY

This game has the potential to be very dangerous. Only do it if the group is working well together and does not deliberately drop the canopy.

MEYNELL

OWN NOTES

AGES

any age

NUMBERS

Min 9 : Ideal 30 : Max ++

ENERGY LEVEL

active

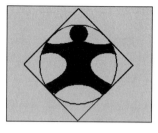

BASIC

One person is selected to be the Eagle and they sit on their perch in the middle of the parachute. The group turns the parachute into the sea by making waves [se earlier] and then 4 people are selected to be fish. With the fish starting at different places under the sea, they have to try to get to the eagle before the eagle catches them. The eagle can only spin around on its perch. The fish can go wherever they like.

SCRIPT

In this game I'm going to look for some more eager, keen, willing participants to put themselves forward as volunteers and firstly I would like an eagle. Now remember an eagle is a vicious, attacking bird of prey that likes eating small things like fish and mice and whatever, so I want someone with a large wing span, ready to come and sit in their perch in the middle of the parachute, and you'll do fine - your name is - Sam, OK Sam the golden eagle, come and sit in the middle, spin on your perch, excellent. Now in this game you are actually sitting on a perch, which could be a tree trunk in the middle of the sea. In the sea are four pretty arrogant fishes and what they are going to try to do is to swim up towards you and nip you before you can eat them. really this is a game of four against one. Who would like to be a fish? Thank you very much you go under there, you go under here, you go under there and you go under there. OK eagle, four fishes starting right at the edge at 12 o'clock, 3 o'clock, 6 o'clock and 9 o'clock. Of course they may go off course, they don't have to swim directly into the middle towards you and you're just going to have to spin around and hope you get all four before they get you and of course fish when you are caught retreat out because that's it it's over and all of the rest of us around the outside can decide whether it's a calm day on this sea with gentle ripples and waves or a stormy day and of course on a stormy day these flying fish may have more of a chance to catch the eagle than on a calm day, so the choice is up to you. Let's go! One fish caught, two fish caught, huh, third fish got the eagle. OK eagle off, fish out and let's do it again.

SAFETY

It's safe so long as the Eagle stays on its perch and the fishes don't get splatted!

MEYNELL

This is a good variation on traditional parachute catch games. Don't stop here — keep making up your own.

OWN NOTES

SECTION 5

TWO PARACHUTE GAMES

If you are fortunate enough to have 2 canopies then these games can add a whole new dimension to your playing experience. Some of the games can be further enhanced with the addition of even more parachutes. The more you've got the bigger the group can get — all you have to decide is how to hold them!

AGES

Any age.

NUMBERS

Min 20 : Ideal 30 : Max ++

ENERGY LEVEL

Hyper/Wild

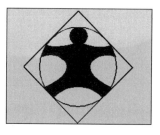

BASIC

This is a two parachute game. Perform as for 'Cat and Mouse' but add a second parachute on top of the first parachute and a dog on top of the second parachute. The mouse is on the floor, cat between the two, and the dog on the top; the dog is chasing the cat, and the cat is chasing the mouse.

SCRIPT

Alright we've got hold of our two parachutes and we need three volunteers. Now in this game it's sensible to hold the big parachute on the ground on the bottom, with our left hand and the small parachute on the top with the right hand. Can I have three volunteers? I'm going to have one person that's a mouse. OK Mouse, you're between the grass and the first one. Cat, who's going to be my cat. No don't put your hands up who's ever seen a cat with their hand in the air. OK Yes, yes, OK you can be my cat and you go between the two, and one more for a dog, I don't want too vicious a dog. Ah, playful puppy, you come on top of this on. Alright. Now, very simple game, the cat has to catch the mouse, and the dog's got to catch the cat. Dog please be careful that you don't tread on the mouse because we would get a squashed mouse and that wouldn't be fun.

SAFETY

Watch out for the knees remind the cat not to splat the mouse and the dog not to splat the cat and the mouse to be careful not to be trodden on.

MEYNELL

OWN NOTES

CAT, MOUSE AND BIRD

AGES

Suitable for mixed age groups but not for the very young ones

NUMBERS

Min 20 : Ideal 30 : Max ++

ENERGY LEVEL

Active

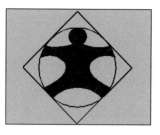

BASIC

In this two parachute game we choose three players: the bird who is on top, the cat in the middle and the mouse on the bottom. The mouse is being chased by both the cat and the bird, the cat is also chasing the bird. All other aspects of the game are as in cat and mouse and cat mouse and dog.

SCRIPT

A bit similar to cat mouse and dog but this time we have the mouse at the bottom, the cat in the middle and the bird on top. Who is going to show me a bird, nice large flapping wings, excellent bird, you are on top, who is going to be my cat? No, I don't want a child with their hand in the air I want a cat. You are a sweet cat, in you come into the middle between the two. Are you OK. in there, yes, and a squeaky mouse. Let's have a large mouse just to confuse things. Now in this game, the cat, you can choose to catch either the bird or the mouse. And to make things even more complicated, the bird, being a bird of prey, likes mice, so the mouse, you are being chased by both the bird and the cat and the cat you are chasing the bird and the mouse . There is no-one chasing the cat as that was last time, and lets shake and go! Yes I know it is confusing, which one are you going for bird? Watch out mouse! Cat, where are you going?! Oh! Cat's got bird, bird's got mouse, all at the same time. Now that really is unusual. OK., off you come, out you come, be careful not to tread on each other, and three more volunteers perhaps?

SAFETY

Make sure that everyone in the game moves carefully so no one will get squashed.

MEYNELL

IF YOU WANT OUR HELP WE ARE ONLY A PHONE CALL AWAY 0181 446 5551

OWN NOTES

AGES

Suitable for mixed age groups but not for the very young ones

NUMBERS

Min 20 : Ideal 30 : Max ++

ENERGY LEVEL

Active

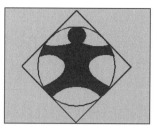

BASIC

Two cats are chosen, one to go on the top parachute and one to go between the two. Two mice are selected, one to go in the middle and one on the bottom. The top cat is chasing the middle mouse and the middle cat is chasing the bottom mouse. As long as the mice are squeaking occasionally the cats stand a chance of catching the correct one.

SCRIPT

This is a double version of Cat and Mouse. We have all played Cat and Mouse, remember?

Now we have two parachutes. So let's get into a circle and pass the parachutes round so that we are all holding both parachutes together. You can either hold them both together or one in each hand, whichever is more comfortable. OK who would like to be the first mouse?

You are under the bottom parachute...cat to chase this one? OK opposite side of the parachutes, in between the two parachutes. You are both going in a clockwise direction. Next mouse, in the middle...cat opposite on top..and you are both going in an anticlockwise direction. OK, remember which one you are trying to catch. Let's go.

Caught them? out you come, more volunteers,....etc.

SAFETY

Ensure that none of the mice get squashed by the cats or by people around the outside.

MEYNELL

Don't stop at two layers — the more parachutes you can lay your hands on the more you can stack up!

OWN NOTES

COGS

AGES

7-8 upwards

NUMBERS

Min 20 : Ideal 40 : Max ++

ENERGY LEVEL

Active/Hyper

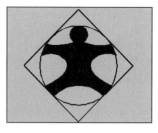

BASIC

This is a two parachute game. The groups spread themselves equally around the edges of the parachutes and imagine themselves to be the spokes on a cog. They start turning the parachute as in 'Walking the Chute'. When this is working the two groups move closer together so that they interlock as cogs at one point.

SCRIPT

Everyone stand up. Let's have two groups, one round each parachute. Hold the parachute with your both hands and pull it until it is tight.

This is not a tug of war we are not trying to pull the people over on the other side. We are just trying to pull it tight. Imagine it as a sheet of steel.

See where the middle is? We are going to try and keep the middle exactly where it is and we are going to walk turning the parachute. We have got to keep the middle where it is. It means thinking about what we are doing and trying to make sure we are all pulling at the same strength. That's good, we have got it going nice and slowly. Now that we know we can do that let's start walking slowly again, but I want each parachute to turn in a different direction, imagine that the parachutes are cogs, and that we are the teeth. What we are going to do is to carry on rotating the cogs and try to get closer to each other so that the teeth on each cog can cog together. Let's move closer and closer and let's see how well we can cog.

SAFETY

A simple and safe exercise as long as nobody walks into anybody else.

MEYNELL

This is another one of Mikes inventions and he has got the video to prove it! We have taken it far since that long day at the Brent Cross Shopping Centre in 1986. We started with two and our current maximum has been six parachutes all cogging happily together at the same time.

OWN NOTES

COG CHANGE

AGES

7-8 upwards

NUMBERS

Min 20 : Ideal 40 : Max ++

ENERGY LEVEL

Active/Hyper

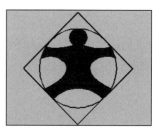

SCRIPT

Now that we are cogging, as we get to the cog point, we are going to change parachutes. It means letting go of the one that you are on and taking hold of the other one, with the other hand. Now that we have this working we can try speeding this up as well. Let's start jogging, running, sprinting, let's slow down, slowly, bit more, a bit more, back to a walk.

Well done! (This is great fun if a little bit complicated...use a s many parachutes as you would like).

BASIC

This is a two parachute game. Perform as 'Cogs' earlier. At the point were the cogs interlock, the person on the edge changes from one canopy to the other.

SAFETY

See safety consideration for cogs.

MEYNELL

Now, if you think this is complicated with two canopies — wait till you get out more and really go for it!

OWN NOTES

IF YOU WANT OUR HELP WE ARE ONLY A PHONE CALL AWAY
0181 446 5551

AGES

Best with older groups

NUMBERS

Min 20 : Ideal 40 : Max ++

ENERGY LEVEL

Hyper

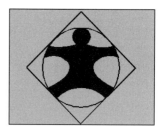

SCRIPT

Let's have a group of people around each parachute. Practice going down and up together to make the parachute billow in the air.

Here is a ball for each parachute...make it bounce...Very good...What I am going to do now is to take one ball away...thank you...now try playing catch.

Toss the ball from one parachute to the other and back again...good (this difficult but not impossible).

Let's try making the ball go higher...Now we can do it with one ball you can have the other ball back and make the balls swap..

Let's go...yeah...wonderful...keep it up...!

BASIC

Have a group of people standing holding on to each parachute. The parachutes should be fairly close together but not touching. Give each parachute a ball and the groups can practise making it bounce and gaining control over the ball. When control has been established, take away one ball and then get the parachute with the ball to throw it so that the other parachute can catch it. They then throw it back again and so on.

SAFETY

A simple and safe exercise,.

MEYNELL

OWN NOTES

CATCH JUGGLING

AGES

Best with older groups

NUMBERS

Min 20 : Ideal 40 : Max ++

ENERGY LEVEL

hyper/wild

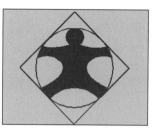

BASIC

This is a follow on from catch. Once the group can pass one ball backwards and forwards to each parachute, add a second ball.

SCRIPT

Now this game takes skill, and working together. You all managed to bounce the ball into the air, and you've managed to pass one ball from one parachute to the other. Now this time there are two balls, one on each parachute and the idea is to get the balls passing from one parachute to the other parachute . So, it's a matter of working together, figuring out how to do it and getting the balls up into the air and cross over and then you catch it on the other parachute like in catch but this time you are both throwing and you are both catching. We've really got this working well - we'll throw in a couple more balls and then I don't know what will happen but we'll all be terribly confused. Off you go! Work together, get the ball up, and over, oh, well one has done it one hasn't, let's get that ball, bring it back onto this parachute, OK., and try again. I never said this would be easy, but it is a matter of skill. Two up, one caught, one falls in the middle, try again! And you've done it, excellent, unbelievable.

SAFETY

Another simple and safe game.

MEYNELL

This is probably one of the hardest to get to work. Even our photo is fixed!!

OWN NOTES

SECTION 6

ULTIMATE CO-OPERATION

Much is written elsewhere in the book about co-operation. These games can bring out the best in a group, but sadly if used at the wrong moment, they can also bring out the worst.

PASSING LEFT LEFT

AGES

Suitable for mixed age groups but not for the very young ones

NUMBERS

Min 15 : Ideal 30 : Max ++

ENERGY LEVEL

Active

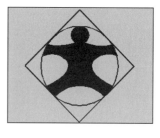

BASIC

The group stand around the edge of the parachute holding it with arms straight down towards the ground and hands slightly apart. A left, right swinging motion is produced as in left right (see earlier). Once the rhythm has been maintained, the parachute is started to be passed from person to person around the side.

SCRIPT

This is a complicated game. A game in which we need to be able to really work together to make it happen. We've done rippling the parachute and we've done left and right with the parachute, remember right at the beginning of the session, we were moving our arms, we had our hands down, and we were swinging our arms and making the parachute go left and right and left and right. OK Let's try doing that again. Everybody, let your arms hang down, keep your arms straight, don't bend them and left and right, left and right. Excellent, now keep that rhythm going whilst I talk to you a bit more. What we've got here is we've got the parachute going backwards and forwards. What we're going to try and do is keep your arms swinging like we are doing at the moment, but pass the parachute to the left as we go . Alright, so left, right, left, right, left, right. Now we have to keep our arms swinging and at the same time pass the parachute on to the left. You've got it. Excellent. Keep that going. Can we get it passing any quicker? Yes that's it. It's really almost just pulling it as you go to the left and letting it high and slide over the edge as they go backwards. That passes it round to the left. Excellent.

Well we seem to have got that. Let's go faster and faster. Brilliant. Alright, can we try doing it the other way.

SAFETY

Be careful of the canopy sliding through your hand, it could cause a burn similar to a rope burn.

MEYNELL

It takes some time to figure this one out but once you've got it, it can be quite fun.

OWN NOTES

IF YOU WANT OUR HELP WE ARE ONLY A PHONE CALL AWAY
0181 446 5551

NAME

WAVE AND BALL

AGES

Suitable for any age, but the under 6's do have some difficulties with it.

NUMBERS

Min 10 : Ideal 30 : Max ++

ENERGY LEVEL

Active/Hyper

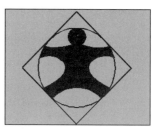

BASIC

The group performs the wave and when this is working successfully a ball is put on to the parachute in front of the wave and the group make the ball pass round the parachute riding on the crest of the wave. Stress to the group to wait for the ball to pass them before they go up with the wave and to keep the wave going fairly calmly.

SCRIPT

What we are going to do now is make the ball travel around the outside of the parachute on the crest of the wave. Stand up, put the ball on the parachute on the edge and if we start with the wave with Sion's left hand, let the ball go around gently, don't touch it with your hands...good. Wait, you have to wait until the ball comes around (roll up the parachute). Go around, go around and stop.

Triffic, o'lrite, now that we can make the wave let's try something a little more complicated. Let's put a ball on..and make it roll..

Remember, wait for the ball to go past before you raise your hand.

We keep the ball on the crest of the wave and watch it roll around the parachute. Let's speed up....let's slow down.

Wonderful!

SAFETY

It is a safe game but you do have to watch out for the ball flying off into people's faces.

MEYNELL

This is almost impossible with a tennis ball, difficult with a football, fun with a 1 metre ball, and totally and utterly brilliant with a 2 metre ball. However if you are going to be using a big 2 metre ball please remember the dangers of an object that size.

OWN NOTES

NAME

ROLL

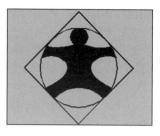

AGES

Suitable for any age, but the under 6's do have some difficulties with it.

NUMBERS

Min 20 : Ideal 30 : Max ++

ENERGY LEVEL

Active

BASIC

The group performs the 'Wave' and one person is selected to ride the wave. They lie on the canopy with their feet towards the centre, their arms stretched out above their heads towards the edge and they are lifted by the parachute wave and rolled around the canopy.

SCRIPT

OK, now in this game I need a volunteer. I'd like to start with a fairly light volunteer if I may, and , well before I choose and of you volunteers, let me tell you what we are going to be doing. Your are going to be lying on the parachute like this, with your feet to the middle and your head out to the side and you arms stretched out above your head. We're going to try rolling you around. Very simple.

So, OK, my volunteer, and your name is Simon. OK Simon, come and lie down, yes that's right take your shoes off and come into the middle and, excellent, lie down, yes you've got that, round a bit, lie down your along one of the lines. Great. Now we are going to try and roll you round. Now the way we do that is everybody takes a little step backwards, with the parachute still flat on the ground, and if the people this side of Simon lift the parachute up, Simon, with a little bit of help from you, you start to roll. As soon as Simon rolls past you lift the parachute up and once he starts rolling you go back down to the ground.

OK, hopefully, the ride is not too bouncy for you Simon, let's go. We've got Simon rolling down, wait for him to come past you then lift the parachute up stretch as high as you can, keep pulling out and as he goes round keep going up and then back down. Excellent, keep him going, keep him going, let's see if we can get him going any faster. Wonderful!

SAFETY

You must be careful that the group do not drop the roller on the ground or cause too many bumps to happen. When it's over be ready to help the roller as they may be dizzy.

MEYNELL

OWN NOTES

NAME

TURN IT OVER

AGES

Suitable for any age

NUMBERS

Min 10 : Ideal 20 : Max ++

ENERGY LEVEL

Calm

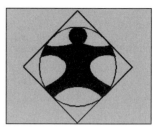

SCRIPT

This is a game of concentration and skill. I'd like you to look where your hands are holding onto the parachute canopy. Now, introduce yourself into this part of the canopy because you are never going to let go, well at least not during this game. At this time, if you look there is a label on the parachute and it is underneath and, you got it, over there on the orange section, good, we are going to turn the parachute so that the label underneath is on the top and you must not let go. I'm not going to give you any more of a clue than that; it's entirely up to you how you do it. Off you go. Alright, a bit confused and a few people have let go. Spread out, you're all messed up in knots, think about how you are going to do this, talk to each other. If you are going to turn it over, some people are going to have to go underneath and some will have to go on top, so make sure whoever is going on top is not wearing shoes and try again.

BASIC

The group stand up around the parachute and are encouraged to not let go of the canopy during this game. The group then needs to identify a difference between the top side and underside of the canopy. The task is to then turn it over without letting go!

SAFETY

Try to do this game calmly without a lot of running or stress.

MEYNELL

Try this game with different ages you will be amazed at the results.

OWN NOTES

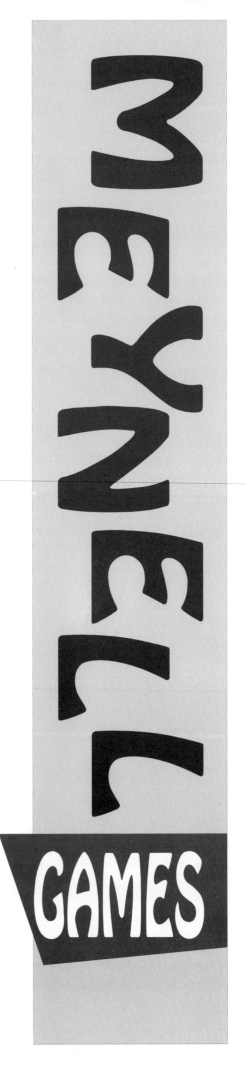

UNDER THE CANOPY

Most of these games are only suitable when working with a fixed group. This is because as soon as you and your participants go under the parachute you become cut off from the outside world. All anyone can see when walking towards you is a strange bubble making funny noises on the floor, and what is even more important is that you don't know that there is anyone out there and cannot invite them to join you.

NAME

TURTLE

NUMBERS

SECTION 7

ENERGY LEVEL

Calm

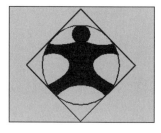

BASIC

The group faces outwards and then steps backwards whilst bringing the parachute over their heads and down in front of them. When the parachute has been pulled forward enough it is placed on the ground and the group kneel on it so that they are underneath the canopy with their bottoms towards the middle and their heads facing to the outside. They then move as a group in a nominated direction, keeping the parachute tight whilst moving.

SCRIPT

Holding onto the parachute, turn round so you are all standing up facing outwards, and now lift the parachute up over your heads and down in front of your nose and walk backwards and pull the parachute down so it is almost in front of your knees, then bend down to the ground and get your knees on the parachute. Now you may have to crawl backwards so your knees are well underneath the parachute so we should all be bottoms into the middle, heads out, knees underneath the parachute. From outside this looks like a turtle shell, so we're going to play some turtle games and the first thing we are going to do is to see if we can all move in the same direction without letting our shell go saggy so let's crawl towards me, I'll lead to begin with. Do you remember there was a tree on the outside, lets crawl towards that tree, and this is good, remember, if you're crawling backwards to crawl slowly so that the parachute stays tight, some people are going to be crawling sideways which is a very interesting concept. OK. let's change direction and go over there then, whoever's leading I don't know, excellent. Quickly duck out because you don't want to get too hot underneath and let's jump up and put some obstacles down. A mat over here, the other parachute over here, a few balls. Now we are going to, as a turtle, go back underneath and try and negotiate our way over these obstacles, and let's go, working together to keep the parachute as a turtle shell.

SAFETY

Some people do not like being under the parachute. Watch out for them. Also beware of the heat factor.

MEYNELL

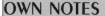

OWN NOTES

SEATED

AGES

Suitable for any age, but best with over 8's

NUMBERS

Min 10 : Ideal 30 : Max ++

ENERGY LEVEL

Calm

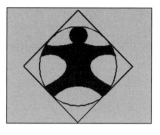

BASIC

Everyone stands up and facing inwards pulls the parachute down behind them, walking forward so that they can sit underneath on the edge of the parachute. Once underneath the canopy a number of different activities such as story telling, joke telling, can take place.

SCRIPT

Stand up, hold onto the parachute, lift your arms up into the air, take a few steps forward and pull the parachute down behind you. Keep walking forwards so the parachutes down behind your bottoms and keep walking forward and then sit down on the parachute. Alright, wriggle forward so that your head is not too stressed and now we can do some gentle rocking, that's good, or remember when we were leaning before in different directions like the aerobics, we can do that, or we could just sit under here and tell a story. Who'd like to tell a story? OK. something a little more energetic to do under here if someone outside would put a ball on top for us, OK. now our task is to keep the ball on top and not loose it over the side which means we want to roll it around so we can all get to touch it, using your feet, carefully lift the parachute up and roll the ball around no, it's off, throw it back on, thank you very much, roll it around try not to kick it - if you do it will fly straight off, stroke it about, let's be gentle. That's nice, we seem to have control of the ball now, can we make it move in a complete circle? Brilliant, how about getting it to drop through the whole in the middle? Ha, ha, excellent, OK. and stop. Calm

SAFETY

This could, if organised poorly, hurt the participants necks. Please be careful.

MEYNELL

OWN NOTES

UNDER THE PARACHUTE

AGES

Any age.

NUMBERS

Min 10 : Ideal 30 : Max ++

ENERGY LEVEL

Active

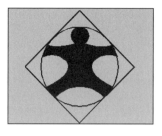

BASIC

As seated except move even further in so that the group is almost lying half supported by the parachute, then put a ball on top. The group then works together to move the ball around but not let it come off.

SCRIPT

OK everyone under the parachute, don't stand up, lift the parachute up...wriggle back so everyone can get round the outside.

Everyone lean back...let your bum slide forward...Have we got anyone on the outside edge of the parachute? Yes, would you like to pick the ball up from the corner and throw it on the parachute...don't let the ball off the parachute...where has the ball gone? OK Co-operation is about getting the ball moving on the outside while we are on the inside.

Alright? Gently push it around the parachute. If we all do it at the same time it is just going to bounce around. Think about the wave...let it move around.

Alright, we have had our five minutes relaxation. Lift the parachute up and get yourselves on the outside.

SAFETY

Check for claustrophobia and make sure that when people are under the parachute the parachute is not pulling on their head in such a way as to strain or sprain their necks.

MEYNELL

OWN NOTES

NAME

TENT POLE

AGES

Any age.

NUMBERS

Min 6 : Ideal 30 : Max ++

ENERGY LEVEL

Mellow

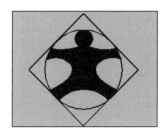

SCRIPT

BASIC

SAFETY

MEYNELL

I know that there is one game called Tentpole, but I have struggled and tried to remember it - but I can't!

OWN NOTES

RELAXING UNDER

AGES

Suitable for any ages, but the under 5's tend just to shake it around.

NUMBERS

Min 10 : Ideal 30 : Max ++

ENERGY LEVEL

Mellow

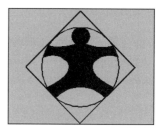

BASIC

Everyone stands holding the parachute and small groups go and lie down underneath. The remainder of the participants gently waft the parachute up and down, letting it gently touch the faces of the people underneath on each down stroke.

SCRIPT

Who would like a nice, cool wafting sort of experience? You would, and you would? OK. those of you with your hands up now that's 8 of you, under you go, lie under the middle, you can lie any way you like, and the rest of us on the outside we are just going to gently and calmly and carefully lift the parachute up and let it come down onto their noses and then up - and gently down, so you're getting a nice waft of fresh calming air under there, and surprisingly we too on the outside are also getting a nice calm, gentle air. OK, that's enough for you underneath, you come out, and swap with others to go underneath, and let's continue.

SAFETY

A gentle and calm activity.

MEYNELL

OWN NOTES

BALL OFF

AGES

Any age.

NUMBERS

Min 14 : Ideal 30 : Max ++

ENERGY LEVEL

Hyper

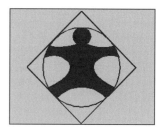

BASIC

The group should already have practised making the ball bounce. Divide the players into two halves on each side of the parachute. The object of the game is for each half to get the ball off over the heads of the people on the other side.

SCRIPT

Who thinks they are in the middle of the parachute on the sides (division of sides). Who has a favourite flavour of ice cream on this side...strawberry, chocolate...this side is going to be chanting strawberry (Try chants). Now the idea for strawberry is to get the ball over the top of the chocolate and chocolate the idea for you is to get the ball over the top of the strawberry.

To do this I will let you into a secret, you have to work together. No touching the ball, use the parachute only. Anyone touching gets walloped by the ball. I am not going to start this off, this is up to you.

Alright stop. Lets go...Stop, stop, stop. OK.

SAFETY

Another simple and fairly safe game, you do have to watch out for the ball coming off and landing on people's heads if they have let go of the edge of the parachute.

MEYNELL

OWN NOTES

NAME

RUSS OFF

AGES

Any age.

NUMBERS

Min 14 : Ideal 30 : Max ++

ENERGY LEVEL

Hyper/Wild

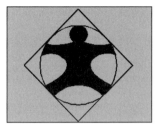

SCRIPT

This is another version of ball off but ball off doesn't have to be played with the ball! We can put anything on top, so who has a friendly little furry chappie, here's Russ. Russ is a bright orange orang-utan and he's a bit wild and crazy and on top you go Russ and shake him around a bit get him use to that. OK. let's find some volunteers to go underneath to push Russ off. Now the idea is to send Russ flying into the air over the heads of people on the outside exactly what we were doing with the ball before, meanwhile all those of us on the outside are going to try and stop Russ from escaping, as once he escapes, who knows what he might do. OK three people going underneath, thank you, you you you and OK. one more let's make it four, try and send Russ flying off. Remember he's a wild creature, you never know what he's going to do, so don't put your hands underneath the parachute, and when underneath don't put your hands through the holes as knowing Russ he'll probably bite them off! Let's play Russ Off! Oh, Russ doesn't appear to be escaping at all. He's there, close to the edge but no, he's flying back towards the middle, let's have a count down from 10, 10 9 8 7 6 5 4 3 2 1

BASIC

This is very similar to ball off!! However, the ball is replaced with a wild furry creature, [who in my games is an orang-utan called Russ] and also some participants who are chosen to go underneath and help push this wild fury creature off.

SAFETY

The biggest danger is that when Russ does manage to get off — you will have no idea haw to catch him and before you know it he'll be after any food that is around!

MEYNELL

Russ is part of my extended family, and I do make sure that before he has a go at this game that I check he is going to be all right and after he comes off he will always get a cuddle. Please treat your little friends with love and affection! Russ also refused to let us photo this game - so I've included one of his holiday snaps!

OWN NOTES

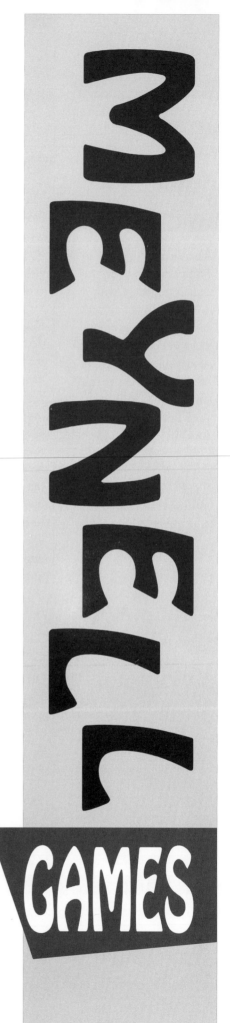

IN THE CANOPY

This is a selection of both gentle and small group games.

AGES

Best for the uner 8's

NUMBERS

Min 5 : Ideal 20 : Max 30

ENERGY LEVEL

Mellow

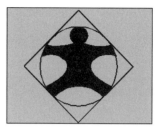

SCRIPT

Put the parachute on the ground. Anyone who is feeling dirty, thinks they need a wash, wants to volunteer, get your shoes off and sit in the middle.

Great sit down. You are the washing. Everyone standing around on the outside are the washers. The parachute is the washing machine. Let's close the washing machine.

OK washers lift the parachute and let's cover the washing. Stand close. Let's pour on some detergent. (mime pouring on detergent). Now let's wash the washing (lean forwards and gently push the washing with your hands and get other washers to follow suit).

This is a delicate/fragile wash so let's wash them carefully. Washing are you done yet? OK let's get the washing out.

Do you see the washing line..look..it's over there! OK Let's hang the washing on the washing line. See it blowing in the breeze. OK washers, the washing line is very heavy...you better go and support it. What a wonderful sight, well done.

BASIC

The parachute is flat on the ground with the group standing around the outside. The group is divided into half, one half selected to sit on the parachute canopy, whilst the other half fold them up in the canopy. After sprinkling in some imaginary washing powder, the group on the outside gently rock and clean the group on the inside. After a period of time the machine (parachute canopy) is opened and the washing is gently taken out and hung up to dry. The groups then change roles.

SAFETY

Make sure that none of the people inside the washing machine are claustrophobic. Ensure that the people on the outside of the washing machine treat the washing gently. This is a gentle game not a vicious game.

MEYNELL

This game and the one on the next page , the Great Escape, were developed at sessions where for one reason or another nearly all our players left us. What were we to do with a parachute and only a few people?

OWN NOTES

NAME

THE GREAT ESCAPE

AGES

Good for all ages

NUMBERS

Min 2 : Ideal 10 : Max 20

ENERGY LEVEL

Mellow

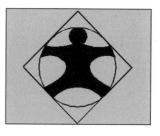

BASIC

The parachute canopy is flat on the ground, a small selected number of people sit on the parachute canopy whilst the others fold the canopy over them and stand around the edges to prevent any escape. The people on the inside then try to find a way out burrowing and pushing until they find an edge.

SCRIPT

This is a game called The Great Escape, and in this game some people are bundled up inside the parachute and others try to prevent them from escaping so who would like to be my escapees? OK volunteer number 1, 2, 3, 4, 5, 6, 7, 8, 9, and 10. Now, you're all going to be bundled up and covered up by the parachute so you'll all be OK in there and none of you are going to get scared? Fine Super.

In you go. Sit down there in the middle and the rest of us lets cover them up. Put that edge over here and this edge of here and that side over here and lets all go round and stand on this loose bit. OK escapees it's your time to try and escape, and as soon as someone gets out of one gap someone on the outside will move round and fill it up so you won't all be able to come out of the same way. OK.

SAFETY

Make sure that none of the people inside are claustrophobic. Ensure that those preventing the escape do so with sensitivity, the aim is eventually let the participants out, not to keep them trapped for the rest of their lives.

MEYNELL

IF YOU WANT OUR HELP WE ARE ONLY A PHONE CALL AWAY
0181 446 5551

OWN NOTES

SIT ON IT

AGES

Any age.

NUMBERS

Min 10 : Ideal 30 : Max ++

ENERGY LEVEL

Mellow/Hyper

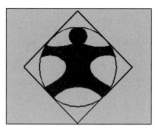

SCRIPT

Who would like to put themselves forward to volunteer to sit in the middle? OK. you would, your name is - Adrian OK. Adrian come and sit in the middle. The rest of us are going to gently waft the parachute up and down at you. We'll step in a bit so the waves will come forward and touch you. Wafting up and down we can do this gently or with a lot more energy. look, he's started to smile! Wave it around, wave, wave, wave, harder and faster and calmer and gently and maybe fast, then slow it down again. OK. and stop.

BASIC

The group is standing gently wafting the parachute and one person goes and sits on top, in the middle. The group then take a step or two forwards and continue to waft sending waves and gusts of air onto the person in the middle. The speed and energy can change depending on the wishes of the person in the middle.

SAFETY

This is designed as a calm game but when played energetically there is the possibility of the canopy flicking the person in the middle.

MEYNELL

OWN NOTES

SIT ON IT VERSION 2

AGES

Any age.

NUMBERS

Min 10 : Ideal 30 : Max ++

ENERGY LEVEL

Mellow/Hyper

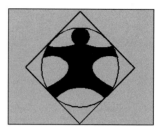

SCRIPT

OK. this time we're going to do the same sort of thing but with balls or balloons in there as well. Tracy, you'd like to volunteer, OK. in you come to the middle, sit down. Lots of balls around, we'll do this calmly to begin with. Tracy watch out for those balls so they don't smack you around too much - -you can catch them and throw them back to the edge, and of course if we didn't have balls we could use balloons which would be a very gentle thing. Maybe a little faster and harder, OK. we can start flipping these around, making it as fast as we like. Tracy, keep your eyes open as balls are coming from everywhere! OK. and stop and someone else would like a go, yes.

BASIC

This is the same as sit on it but with the addition of either small balls or balloons. The person in the middle can then pat these away from them or catch them end throw the towards the edge.

SAFETY

When the balls start flying around they can pick up quite a fast speed. The person in the middle could also get a little too excited and start throwing the balls at the people shaking the canopy who in turn might start throwing them back.

MEYNELL

Whilst most people have easy access to balls and would use them for this game, balloons are truly wonderful. If it a hot day and you are outdoors and you have got a fairly good group — try water balloons!

OWN NOTES

IF YOU WANT OUR HELP WE ARE ONLY A PHONE CALL AWAY 0181 446 5551

SECTION 9

ADVANCED GAMES

The games in this section require a lot of people working well together whom you trust. Some are complex in organisation and others require sensitivity and a certain skill level from the group.
They are all, however, good closing games at large outdoor events.

NAME

ROLL CHASE

AGES

Suitable for any age, but the under 6's do have some difficulties with it.

NUMBERS

Min 20 : Ideal 30 : Max ++

ENERGY LEVEL

Active

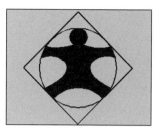

BASIC

The group performs 'Roll' but this time two people are selected who start at opposite sides of the canopy and the group around the outside try to make one person catch up with the other.

SCRIPT

This time I want two volunteers. We're going to start with each of you on opposite sides of the parachute and we're going to try and make one of you catch the other. So we can make one person roll and now we're going to try doing it with two, so let's get two people in place, yes excellent, you over there and you over here, that's really good. Lie down stretch your arms out and remember your going to have to help, we'll start off rolling in a clockwise direction and as the parachute comes up you two lying on it give them a bit of a help by starting to roll.

OK, on the count of three we'll get going, one, two, three, go. Let's roll let's try and catch them up. Oh, number one is catching number two, the gaps closing, no, number two's speeding up again. Keep it going, keep it going, keep it going, excellent! Alright and stop, now stand up both of you very, very carefully, if they ;look dizzy people on the side jump in and support them so that they don't fall over.

SAFETY

The same considerations as for Roll but also make sure that if one player catches the other, they don't end up being churned around together.

MEYNELL

OWN NOTES

TURN AND WALK

AGES

Suitable for any age, but better with older groups.

NUMBERS

Min 20 : Ideal 30 : Max ++

ENERGY LEVEL

Active/Hyper

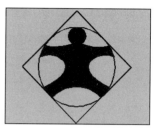

BASIC

The group perform 'Round in Circles' whilst one selected person stands on top and walks in the opposite direction. The selected person may choose to stand either near the apex or near the edge or anything in between.

SCRIPT

Let's have a volunteer. Shoes off, come and stand on the parachute. We are going to turn the parachute one way and you are going to walk the other. You ready? Let's try it.

Do you remember how we were holding onto the parachute canopy with one hand and walking in a circle? Let's just remember yes we can do that and we can walk, jog, run, whatever. Now what we are going to do is have one other person who's is going to be on top of the canopy going in the opposite direction. Who would like to do this? And your name is - Becky, alright Becky on you come, we'll start off slowly Becky, if you keep towards the outside edge then you'll find yourself up in the air rather than on the ground. Let's walk, and we'll speed up so we are walking quickly, and the idea is Becky that you walk in the opposite direction that we're walking in and you walk at the same speed as us. Let's jog, and let's jog faster, let's run, and let's sprint, keeping it tight, and let's slow it down, slow it down, slow it down, walk, walk, and stop. Becky, you're a little bit dizzy, let's help you off there, carefully, down to the ground, let Becky off, and thank you.

SAFETY

As round in circles in itself has the potential to really damage the participants, when combined with someone on top the risk factor is doubled. Only do this if you are confident, and your group is experienced, responsible and strong.

MEYNELL

OWN NOTES

NAME

TRAMPOLINING

AGES

Any age.

NUMBERS

Min 10 : Ideal 30 : Max ++

ENERGY LEVEL

Active

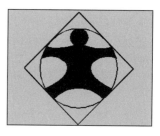

BASIC

The group performs 'Mushroom' but one person is selected to lie in the centre of the canopy and is mushroomed into the air.

SCRIPT

OK I want one volunteer someone who is willing, very willing in fact to come and lie in the middle of this parachute canopy. OK Thank you very much, your name is? OK France come and lie down over here. Now you're going to lie in the middle and the rest of us are going to lift the parachute up and send you flying. Are you OK about that? Do you still want to do this? Yes Good. Are you sure? Because you can change your mind if you don't want to. No, you do want to. OK you lie there and I'll go back to the sides. OK, now everybody remembers how we did the mushroom, I go One, Two, Three UP we all go on the UP, stand up and stretch our hands high above our heads and this time when we do it Francine gets a free ride and we turn the parachute into a trampoline and send her flying into the air. Everybody ready, OK One, Two, Three, UP and gently lower her back done to the ground.

SAFETY

Make sure the group is safe and won't drop the person on the floor.

MEYNELL

IF YOU WANT OUR HELP WE ARE ONLY A PHONE CALL AWAY 0181 446 5551

OWN NOTES

EGG TOSS

Any age.

NUMBERS

Min 10 : Ideal 30 : Max ++

ENERGY LEVEL

Active

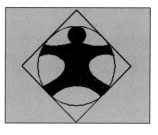

SCRIPT

OK This time I would like a volunteer to come and do exactly the same as last time but sitting in the middle. Oh, I can't choose everybody so let's just choose one person so I'll choose you, your name is .. Emma. OK, Emma, now Emma come and sit in the middle, right over the centre, hold on to the strings if you want to. I'll get off back round the side, everybody ready...one, two, three, UP.

BASIC

This is the same as trampolining but with one person sitting.

SAFETY

Make sure the group is safe and won't drop the person on the floor.

MEYNELL

OWN NOTES

NAME

HIGH IN THE SKY

AGES

Any age.

BASIC

This is the same as trampolining but with one person standing.

NUMBERS

Min 20 : Ideal 30 : Max ++

ENERGY LEVEL

Active

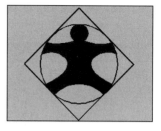

SCRIPT

Alright we're going to take trampolining and egg toss one stage further. This time I'd like a willing volunteer who is not going to lie in the middle or sit in the middle, but who is going to stand in the middle. OK, you are my chosen one come with me, what's your name, OK Arturo, what I would like you to do is to stand in the middle, your feet just on the rim, there where the strings join the parachute, Excellent. Now bend your knees slightly as if you were skiing because you probably will fall over, but we'll keep the parachute tight so that you won't fall and hit the ground. Well I hope not anyway. One, Two, Three UP, Excellent!

SAFETY

Make sure the group is safe and won't drop the person on the floor and that the person in the middle is happy about what is going on.

MEYNELL

OWN NOTES

SECTION 10

MORE GAMES

Fitting games into categories has been a very hard task, but these ones I just couldn't figure out. I know that some games seem to be in the wrong section, so to avoid any further confusion all those that were left — went here!!

NAME

MOUSETRAP

AGES

Good for all ages

NUMBERS

Min 15 : Ideal 30 : Max ++

ENERGY LEVEL

Hyper

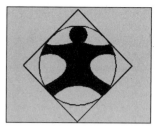

BASIC

The group work the same as they do in Colour Change, but as soon as the colour has been called out, one person counts to ten and as soon as they get to ten, everybody who is not changing places underneath pulls the parachute canopy back down to the ground. Then they quickly lift it up to release those people trapped.

SCRIPT

OK. What we are going to do now is to take Colour Change one stage further. We've all been going One, Two, Three, IGLOO and I've been calling out a category and everybody has been running underneath and changing places. What we are going to now is as soon as I call out what ever it is I'm going to call out, I'm going to count to ten. As soon as I count to ten, all of those who aren't running are going to pull the parachute back down to the ground as quickly as they can. This is a game that we call Mousetrap and I think the reason is obvious. So, how fast can I count to ten? (little voice 1,2,3,4,5,6,7,8,9,10. OK thank you). Can anyone demonstrate a quicker count than that. 1,2,3,4,6,7,9,10. Yes but you need to put all the numbers in. (couple more demonstrations) Excellent!

Alright, everybody down to the ground, down to the ground. Knees bent, bottom off the ground, holding on to the edge, don't forget to shout IGLOO, one, two, three, IGLOO! Everybody who had weetabix for breakfast! 1,2,3,4,5,6,7,8,9,10, down to the ground. OK, lift it up and let them out. Quickly out, quickly, quickly, quickly out. Hold on to the edge, down to the ground, let's do it again. One, two, three, IGLOO! Everybody who hates Neighbours, 1,2,3,4,5,6,7,8,9,10, down to the ground. OK lift it up. Let them out. No lift it out let them out. Don't keep them under there too long. Excellent and down to the ground. Let's do it a couple more times. One , two, three IGLOO, anyone with short hair, 1,2,3,4,5,6,7,8,9,10. Down to the ground. OK lift it up, let them out.

SAFETY

Remind the participants that if they dive out the ground isn't bouncy. Outside they can get grass burns, inside the ground is just painful. Also remind people to watch out for diving into legs of the people standing on the outside and warn of any other objects in the area that they could run into or dive into.

MEYNELL

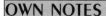

OWN NOTES

AEROBICS

AGES

7-8 upwards

NUMBERS

Min 15 : Ideal 30 : Max ++

ENERGY LEVEL

Active/Hyper

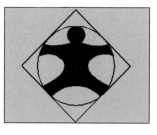

BASIC

The group sit on the ground with their feet underneath the parachute, arms bent, elbows dug into the waist and wriggle back as far as they can so that the parachute is tort. Define four equally spaced points around the parachute, A being opposite C, B being opposite D. On the instruction A, those in the A region lean backwards pulling those in the C region to lean forwards, B and D going from side to side. On calling C, C lean backwards, A lean forwards. Likewise with B and D. When this is established, the call can become A, B, C, D, with each section leaning back in turn, pulling others forwards or sideways. This could be done slowly or quickly.

SCRIPT

Sit down, feet under the parachute. OK Relax. Now pull the parachute. Wriggle back until the parachute is tight. Don't pull the people over who are opposite you. We just want a nice flat tight parachute.

Now let's imagine the parachute is a sheet of steel. Absolutely solid and we are linked by it. Now if I lean backwards, the people opposite me are going to have to lean forwards because they are going to find themselves falling that way, the people at the sides are going to find themselves leaning sideways.

Sit up. I have never seen steel with ripples in it before. Let's keep it tight. The people opposite me lean backwards then us over this side will have to lean forwards. Let's allow ourselves to be pulled by the parachute.

Sit up. This is not being very fair on the people at the sides. What we are going to try and do is rather than just going backwards and forwards we are going to swing our bodies in a circle. This means everyone will have the opportunity of going backwards, forwards and sideways. Are you ready. Let's swivel.

When you go back, really try to get your head down on the ground. Stretch forwards as far as you can go. This is great. Can you feel the inches coming off your waist. Let's try and move faster and faster. OK. Let's die!

SAFETY

There is a possibility for people to hit their head on the ground if they are not careful and the potential also exists for the participants to get very dizzy.

MEYNELL

OWN NOTES

NAME

LEANING

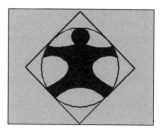

AGES

7-8 upwards

NUMBERS

Min 15 : Ideal 30 : Max ++

ENERGY LEVEL

Calm

BASIC

The group stand around the edge of the parachute holding it with their arms bent, their elbows locked into their waists, and feet slightly apart. On the instruction of lean, the group will lean outwards together, thus supporting each others' weight. One person should count one, two, three and everybody calls lean as they lean backwards. The parachute will become tight holding everybodys weight.

SCRIPT

OK, everybody stand up, let your arms hang loose. Move back a little bit so it's fairly tight. Alright, I'd like you to stand with your feet apart and your elbows bent and your elbows digging in to your sides, a bit like I'm doing. OK, so kind of like with your arms with a 90 degree angle to themselves. Alright, now we've got a little bit of slack in the middle of the parachute and what's going to happen is I'm going to count, 1, 2, 3, , lean and on the word lean I want you all to just lean backwards, keeping your arms bent. The parachute will go tight and nobody will fall over. Aright, you understand? Good. 1, 2, 3, LEAN. Excellent! Now the problem is we've all got to stand up together because otherwise the parachute will fall over. 1, 2, 3, up. good. Now, everyone take a little step forwards, which means we're going to be leaning a bit further. 1, 2, 3, LEAN. 1, 2, 3, UP. Excellent. You have to try to think that their is a wooden plank tied from your ankles, your hips, your chest, so your body stays in a straight line as you lean. If you want to be a bit more adventurous, as you lean backwards, let your arms straighten out, rather than keeping them bent. OK> Let's try that. 1, 2, 3, LEAN. Excellent.

Alright, do want to try taking a step further forwards? Good, alright we've got quite a deep bucket in front of us now which means that we're going to be leaning back a long way, so be careful, that you don't slip or anything. 1, 2, 3, LEAN. Quickly 1, 2, 3, UP, alright a few people fell over there, try that again and really try to let your whole body go backwards. OK.

Try to keep your feet still and trust people around the parachute. We will all support each other.

OK 1 2 3 LEAN!

SAFETY

Watch out for the participants feet slipping on the surface that you are using, for people leaning before the instruction to lean is given and for one side of the parachute being much heavier with the people around it than the other side and therefore, that side falling over.

MEYNELL

OWN NOTES

NAME

STORY TIME

AGES

Any age.

NUMBERS

Min 2 : Ideal 30 : Max ++

ENERGY LEVEL

Calm/Active

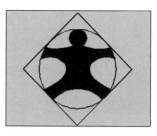

SCRIPT

Are you feeling tired? Yes? OK Sit down, let me tell you a story (if no OK hold the parachute tight, I am going to tell you an exciting story).

Imagine a nice sunny day out on a calm sea, a light breeze wafting through the almost still warm air. Little ripples on the wave (follow words with action with the parachute, the group will follow, its magic, they always do). Little ripples, lots of little ripples.

The wind begins to rise, the waves are getting stronger, sky is getting darker...the blue sea is turning darker...the wind begins to howl (everyone howl??) the waves are becoming choppy...little white caps appear on the waves..it's very choppy...beginning to blow up a storm, eight foot waves, ten foot waves, twenty foot waves, enormous footage of waves (it's quite fun doing this bit, everyone throws the parachute into the air and jumps after it ...)

The rain is pouring down now, lightning flashes, thunder roars, the skies look like they are trying to become part of the water, the sea is rolling around all over the place...suddenly an enormous, unbelievable, amazing, mighty thunder clap rips through the air and everything goes..   ..still.

BASIC

The group sits around the sides of the parachute. One person tells a story, the other people move the parachute in time with the story.

SAFETY

This is a simple and safe exercise.

MEYNELL

The script that I have used here is really quite boring! Be imaginative, look for new stories and develop a whole new process of story telling and using the parachute at the same time. When you've done it — send me some of your stories please!

OWN NOTES

NAME

OVER THE MOUNTAIN

AGES

Good for all ages

NUMBERS

Min 10 : Ideal 30 : Max ++

ENERGY LEVEL

Active/Hyper

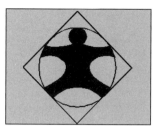

BASIC

The group perform the 1, 2, 3, UP and then on the instruction down bring the parachute back to the ground. A small hump is formed in the middle. By taking small steps forward whilst repeating this exercise, eventually a sizeable mountain will be made by the air caught underneath. When the group have established this, and if they have their shoes off, they can them play 'colour change' but over the top!

SCRIPT

OK time to do something different. Remember how we did the 1, 2, 3, up at the beginning of the session? Good! This time as soon as you go up I'll call out down and you bring the parachute back to the ground. Ready? 1, 2, 3, UP, DOWN. OK stand up and take a small step forwards, let's do it again, 1, 2, 3, UP< DOWN. Stand up and another step forwards and when we do it this time the hump in the middle will get bigger, 1, 2, 3, UP, DOWN. Now we have created a big mountain filled with air and this time as soon as we go down I will call out a colour and if you are wearing that colour, stand up and go over the mountain to the other side. Be careful of the holes and watch out as the mountain will collapse under you!

Ready and 1, 2, 3, UP, DOWN, yellow!

SAFETY

The dangers are tripping over the billowing material, jumping on to the mountain and crashing on to the ground, running into each other, and tripping over the strings/holes of the canopy.

MEYNELL

This creates as much laughter and excitement as does the traditional mushroom!

OWN NOTES

IF YOU WANT OUR HELP WE ARE ONLY A PHONE CALL AWAY 0181 446 5551

Index 1

FINAL WORDS

Thank you for buying my book -- and for reading it! I hope that you have found it useful and have enjoyed your playing.

I plan to publish updates from time to time and in this I ask your help. We all alter and develop games, sometimes this is prompted by the participants and at other times we just have excellent ideas. I know that I would like to try your ideas with my groups and I expect that many other playworkers would also like to share and learn new ideas and games.

Please send me your games so that I can then include them in Parachute Play -- Volume 2. I will try to include an acknowledgement of their origination in the next book.

During the next year it is my intention to produce some other books in which I hope you will be interested. There will be a book on the practicalities of setting up a holiday playscheme. This book, called 'Meynell Games on. . .Holiday Playschemes', focuses on the programmes, activities and logistics of the playscheme. There will also be books of art, crafts, and physical play ideas and a book on using 1 metre and 2 metre balls.

If you wish to be kept informed please write to me and I will keep your name and interests on file.

Thank you.